Mindfulness Meditation

How to Completely Destroy Stress and Anxiety in Some Days

(Letting Go of Worry and Depression and Empowering Yourself to Reach a State of Enlightenment)

Edwin Aube

Published by Rob Miles

© **Edwin Aube**

All Rights Reserved

Mindfulness and Meditation: How to Completely Destroy Stress and Anxiety in Some Days (Letting Go of Worry and Depression and Empowering Yourself to Reach a State of Enlightenment)

ISBN 978-1-989990-95-7

All rights reserved. No part of this guide may be reproduced in any form without permission in writing from the publisher except in the case of brief quotations embodied in critical articles or reviews.

LEGAL & DISCLAIMER

The information contained in this book is not designed to replace or take the place of any form of medicine or professional medical advice. The information in this book has been provided for educational and entertainment purposes only.

The information contained in this book has been compiled from sources deemed reliable, and it is accurate to the best of the Author's knowledge; however, the Author cannot guarantee its accuracy and validity and cannot be held liable for any errors or omissions. Changes are periodically made to this book. You must consult your doctor or get professional medical advice before using any of the suggested remedies, techniques, or information in this book.

Upon using the information contained in this book, you agree to hold harmless the Author from and against any damages, costs, and expenses, including any legal fees potentially resulting from the application of any of the information provided by this guide. This disclaimer applies to any damages or injury caused by the use and application, whether directly or indirectly, of any advice or information presented, whether for breach of contract, tort, negligence, personal injury, criminal intent, or under any other cause of action.

You agree to accept all risks of using the information presented inside this book. You need to consult a professional medical practitioner in order to ensure you are both able and healthy enough to participate in this program.

Table of Contents

INTRODUCTION 1

CHAPTER 1: MINDFULNESS EXPLAINED – WHAT IS MINDFULNESS? 7

CHAPTER 2: PRACTICING MINDFULNESS 17

CHAPTER 3: INTRO TO COGNITIVE RESTRUCTURING 27

CHAPTER 4: MEDITATION CAN HELP YOU ACHIEVE YOUR GOAL 36

CHAPTER 5: OVERCOMING NEGATIVE THOUGHTS MINDFULLY 41

CHAPTER 6: MINDFULNESS EXERCISES FOR BEGINNERS .. 45

CHAPTER 7: MINDFULNESS MEDITATION IN DEPTH 50

CHAPTER 8: THE PRACTICE OF MINDFULNESS AND MEDITATION. 67

CHAPTER 9: TECHNIQUES AND PRACTICE 71

CHAPTER 10: BODY SCAN MEDITATION 78

CHAPTER 11: SIMPLE TIPS FOR BEING MORE MINDFUL EVERYDAY 82

CHAPTER 12: GAIN UNDERSTANDING AND SELF-AWARENESS 89

CHAPTER 13: LET'S PRACTICE 95

CHAPTER 14: CLEAR YOUR ENERGY 101

CHAPTER 15: HOW MINDFULNESS CAN HELP? 116

CHAPTER 16: HAVE A MIND OF YOUR OWN 135

CHAPTER 17: THE THREE POISONS 139

CHAPTER 18: MINDFULNESS TECHNIQUE #3: CURATING YOUR THOUGHTS 148

CHAPTER 19: BELIEF SYSTEM EXERCISE.......................... 159

CHAPTER 20: THE BAD AND UGLY 162

CHAPTER 21: MINDFULNESS ALL DAY AND EVERY DAY . 168

CHAPTER 22: EMOTIONAL MEDITATION 188

CONCLUSION.. 202

Introduction

If you haven't heard of mindfulness, then I assume you don't read much or keep up with the latest news in healthcare. Many people are dealing with the effects of stress. In fact, the numbers are so worryingly high that medical experts in the field admit that current treatment isn't really addressing the problem. In this book, I will show you scientifically and medically why mindfulness meditation works. There will be no two ways about it. By the time that the book is finished, you will know it to be fact.

Acting on what you learn, you will find that you become a more compassionate, patient, and better person if you follow the instructions that are given in the book because there is absolutely no scientific reason why that should not happen. In the first part of the book, I will go over a little about the history and also explain why medical experts also agree that mindfulness meditation works. You will be given full instructions on how to do this on a daily basis, and the choice and the responsibility are left in your hands. However, if you choose to go this route, you will find that your life becomes easier. You will find that the stress dissipates, and that anxiety is something from the past. Is it really that effective? The truth is that it is, and all it takes is a little willing from you to make mindfulness meditation something that becomes part of your life. When you do, things change drastically, and you no longer respond to life with the same anxiety.

Many years ago, I believed that it couldn't work or that people were tagging onto a new kind of phase. I believed in the logic of life that I had been taught but had no idea of the power of mindfulness. When I introduced it into my life, I found there was a calm that I had not experienced for many years, and my life has been like that ever since. I have been teaching mindfulness meditation for a very long time, and it has changed my life entirely. I did it through choice, and students that learn with me are either there by choice, or they learn nothing. You see, it's a case of adopting a lifestyle, rather than simply doing something and then not doing it. Mindfulness follows you in everything that you do, and when you do it on a daily basis, it becomes part of who you are.

Meditation allows you to link your mind to your body, and although it's physically linked already, often, you don't listen to the needs of the body or understand the physiology of the body. And that's important to learn, which is why I have included it in the book. The needs of a human being vary from person to person, but mindfulness gets past that individuality and is able to help anyone who wants to be helped.

The fact that you have picked up this book and read this introduction tells me that you are comparing books on the subject, deciding which one to buy. That's okay, too, as although there are those who may scrutinize my words, that's fine. The way that I have written the book, although simple in form, is so the majority can gain from it without having to understand too much about the religious side of meditation. It's not just yogis and monks who meditate. Many other people do too. The late, great Leonard Cohen was a great believer in meditation and lived a very humble and satisfying life based upon what he believed and being able to put this together with his very personal belief in the Jewish faith. Mindfulness does not demand that you step aside from your beliefs. It merely helps you to make the link complete between your body and your mind to find a higher version of who you are, that doesn't allow stresses and strains of life to touch the course that he is on. It makes you mentally strong without being tough. It makes you thoughtless and compassionate and embraces all of the good things in life. It increases your appreciation of life so that you can go forward with a much more positive attitude.

The positive attitude that you gain through mindfulness meditation also makes you a stronger person who can face adversity in the future and come through it relatively unscathed. That doesn't mean that you won't experience sadness, and sadness is a natural contrast to feeling euphoric. What you haven't learned yet is that everything starts and ends with how your mind perceives it. And that is where mindfulness is lodged – in mind and in the actions of the person who has learned it. I am so impressed by the results that I was able to fight off the fact that my genetics were not too clever and that I may just have been predisposed toward ailments that I have avoided with the use of mindfulness meditation. I am also thrilled to be given this opportunity to share what I know with the public because once you know and believe in Mindfulness Meditation, you will be sure to share the experience with people that you know need it. As people become more aware of what they can do for themselves to help overcome stress in their lives, the world becomes a better and more compassionate place. Let mindfulness wake up your senses and start to trust your intuition once again, against the noise of a technologically advanced society, and you will find that you are able to overcome the stressful problems that life in the 21st century presents to you through following the exercises presented in the book.

Chapter 1: Mindfulness Explained – What Is Mindfulness?

Before we can learn how to practice mindfulness, it is important that we first understand what mindfulness is and what it entails. Mindfulness can be described as the 'basic human capacity to be present in the fullest.' By being mindful, you are aware of where you are and what you are doing. You are rarely overly reactive or overwhelmed by things and happenings around you. This way, you can be said to be fully in control of your environment and present circumstances.

With mindfulness, it becomes possible, even easy, to live in the "now'. This is not to say that if you practice mindfulness, you are not prone to drifting away; you are just as susceptible as anyone else. However, you can bring yourself back to reality over and over again, until the bulk of your thoughts focus on the present.

The best thing about mindfulness is that it is something that each human being already possesses. It is not something that you have to learn and build from scratch. You were born with mindfulness; you just buried it under stacks and stacks of worry, brooding, anticipation, and over-reaching.

While the quality of mindfulness is innate, the reality is that you can add to it – or cultivate it – via proven techniques. The best of them include walking, seated, standing, and moving meditation. You could also meditate while lying down, but the problem with this one is that many people tend to drift off to sleep. This book will show you how to meditate as well as expound on the benefits you get to reap from constant meditation later in the book.

Meditation, at its finest, can be incorporated into every activity that you do. What does this mean? Well, you can take short pauses, be it at work, while playing sports, while doing yoga, etc. to meditate.

A minute or two is enough to reset you to the present state. In fact, we might say that the very crux of meditation is "la pausa," which is the Spanish philosophy of "deliberate, steady pauses in an activity meant to reinforce deliberateness, control and the present as a whole."

When you meditate, it will help you if you focus on the practice rather than being fixated on the benefits that you expect. For one, you will very likely not see the benefits of meditation tomorrow, or the day after. But they will come, by and by. Just by being mindful, you cut down on your stress levels, your heart rate goes down, and you instantly enhance your performance. You also gain insight and awareness, and your powers of observation improve.

Mindfulness meditation also enables you to suspend judgment and substitute it with natural, constructive curiosity. Rather than being closed off mentally (and thus prone to ignorance), you will be eager to learn more and to understand. This will make you a better person, and it will do a lot to improve your relationships with others.

8 Things You Need to Know About Mindfulness:

Mindfulness is not an obscure or exotic quality. Anybody trying to sell you this angle is telling you a lie. Mindfulness is familiar to you, and this has been the case since you were a kid.

Mindfulness isn't something special, or some added thing that we do. We can already be in the present. You do not require reconfiguring who you are to be present or mindful. However, you can cultivate these innate elements that prop up mindfulness and living in the present. You do this via simple practices like meditation. You take short pauses to reflect and reset your concentration on the present.

You do not need to change or revise your personality. Look at history. Look at your own history, even. The solutions that worked best are those that encouraged you to be yourself and break down problems while in your element. Solutions that asked you to revise your nature very likely failed badly. Mindfulness recognizes and cultivates the best versions of ourselves.

Mindfulness can be a transformative social quality. Here's why/how:

Anybody can practice mindfulness. Mindfulness focuses primarily on universal human qualities. It does not call for you to change your religion or your beliefs. No matter who you are, you can practice mindfulness. Everyone stands to benefit and what is more; mindfulness is easy to learn.

Mindfulness is a lifestyle. It is a way of living, as opposed to being just a practice. It 'invites' awareness and care into the things that we choose to do. It dissipates needless tension and stress. Even a little mindfulness will instantly make your life better.

Mindfulness is evidence-based. You do not have to take mindfulness at face value or on faith. Science has proven that mindfulness is beneficial and that meditation has significant physical and psychological benefits. This book will expound on these at a later chapter. Being mindful positively impacts your work, happiness, and relationships.

Mindfulness sparks innovation. In a world where things keep getting increasingly complex, mindfulness helps you truly glean and respond, rather than react, to seemingly intransigent problems.

One of the best ways to cultivate mindfulness is to incorporate meditation into your life. The following chapter focuses on meditation and explains what it really is and its relationship with mindfulness

Meditation Explained- What is Meditation?

What is meditation?

Meditation is a mental exercise that involves relaxing, focusing and ultimately being aware. The practice is to the mind what physical exertion and exercise are to the body. Usually, people stay still (often seated) while meditating. However, you can meditate while walking, moving, standing, etc. Different strokes for different people and all that.

How does psychology define meditation?

You can practice meditation in 1 of 3 modes:

Concentration: This involves focusing your attention on a singular object. The object could be internal or external, and this is focused attention meditation.

Observation: This involves paying attention to the thing that is predominant in your experience, at least in the present moment. You do this without allowing your attention to get stuck to any particular object or thing; this is open-monitoring meditation.

Awareness: Here, you allow awareness to stay present. You remain undistracted and disengaged with either observation or focusing.

Some characteristics of meditation include:

The practice is, at its core, an individual practice. Even when done in groups, it remains inherently personal.

When performing still/seated meditation, it is best to keep your eyes closed. The reason is that you are better able to stave off distractions.

Meditation primarily involves bodily stillness. If you have to make movements, such as in walking/working meditation, make them subtle so as not to disrupt the process.

Here are some other definitions of meditation:

In Christianity, meditation is a type of 'contemplative prayer' whose purpose is to build a sense of union with God.

Meditation is also defined as the contemplation of and reflection on religious themes.

In Buddhism, meditation makes one-third of the core set of practices for mind purification and the attainment of Nirvana. Nirvana refers to a 'perfect sense of enlightenment and mastery over self.'

So, what else does meditation involve?

Besides focus and awareness, meditation heavily involves mental calmness. It involves introspection, which entails 'looking within.' As such, meditation is somewhat different compared to such spiritual exercises as:

Affirmation, guided visualization or self-hypnosis – Here, the goal is to brand a specific message on the mind

Pure relaxation – The goal here is to dispel bodily tensions

Prayer – While there is a conscious flow of feeling and thought, the ultimate objective is to bond with a deity.

Contemplation - The thought process is deeply and actively engaged in sharpening and deepening the understanding of a particular concept or subject.

Trance dancing – The main goal here is to push the practitioner into an altered state of consciousness and perhaps stimulate visions.

While all these practices are good in themselves and certainly helpful, the truth is that they are different from meditation. Many people make the mistake of linking them to meditation or believing they are a form of meditation. The truth is that they aren't. However, there are meditation techniques that borrow some elements from these practices.

Let us evaluate some basics of mindfulness now, as you get started with practicing mindfulness.

Chapter 2: Practicing Mindfulness

"Philippians 4:6-7; Do not be anxious about anything, but in everything by prayer and supplication with thanksgiving let your requests be made known to God. And the peace of God, which surpasses all understanding, will guard your hearts and your minds in Christ Jesus."

•Mindfulness can be precarious from the outset. Our minds are accustomed to meandering, and we will regularly be enticed to fix on an idea or an inclination, judge it as positive or negative, or make a solid effort to break down or transform it. Sometimes this will be valuable, yet we additionally have the option to sit with our experience and be fully aware at that moment, without being hauled away by thoughts or feelings that may do harm in the event if they hang on for a really long time.

In all actuality, the only place we can completely be is at this very moment.

Obviously, it is imperative to plan the future or reflect on the past, however it's about parity.

15 On the off chance that you haven't practiced mindfulness previously, attempt to supplant any judgment you may have about whether you're doing something appropriately, with affirmation that you are doing the absolute best you can at the time. What's significant is that you are doing it. The rest will come with practice. The more you practice mindfulness, the simpler it will move toward becoming to remain present and concentrate on where you need it, instead of dwelling on any place your mind may take you.

Keep in mind additionally that mindfulness is dose-related. The more you do it, the more you will profit by it. The most significant thing is to begin, and to move in the direction of a regular act of at least twenty minutes every day. On the off chance that twenty minutes is hard to discover, and in some cases it very well may be, go after two brief sessions. Here are some various approaches to practice mindfulness:

1. Devote time and space for your mindfulness practice.

You need the space to decide for mindfulness practice to be peaceful, quiet, and calming. You will likewise need to pick a period during which you are probably not going to be intruded. Make a space in your home that is quiet and enables you to simply unwind while practicing mindfulness. Try not to utilize this space for anything beside meditating. Along these lines, when you plunk down, your body will be advised that the time has come to quiet down and practice mindfulness.

2. Attempt to concentrate on the present moment, without judgment.

Looking at the situation objectively, the only moment wherein you are extremely ready to live is the present. Try not to consider the future or the past, and completely acknowledge yourself at the time. Continuously return to concentrating on your breath and tuning in to the sounds around you.

3. Enable you to sit idle and simply be.

You don't generally need to go around so as to get things achieved. Frequently, your mind and body need to revive so you can be profitable when you need to work. Enable yourself to have this resting period, and consider it a fundamental part of carrying on with a good life over the long haul.

4. Try not to consider the past. Try not to plan for the future. Try not to take a look at the time.

You realize you can't change the past. So for what reason wouldn't you be able to let it go? Quit pondering about things that have just occurred. Moreover, what's to come isn't here yet, so there is no effective reason to concentrate too eagerly on that either. The future will come to you soon enough. Concentrate rather on the present moment without stressing over what time it is, or when you must be some place next. Try not to stress over how much time you permit to pass before getting up. It can be connected to

Proverbs 4:23; Keep your heart with all vigilance, for from it flow the springs of life.

5. Focus on your thoughts, words, activities, and inspirations.

When you are thinking, saying, or accomplishing something, what is the purpose for it? It is safe to say that you are recounting to somebody a story to profit him in some way, or is it simply profiting you or your conscience? Consider the inspirations driving all that you do before you do it to check whether it is extremely vital. Ensure that you are continually coming from a good place when you talk or act in any way.

6. Notice your judgements and let them pass.

It is alright to have judgements. This is a natural thing that everybody encounters.

In any case, it is imperative to recognize them and enable them to go as just momentary considerations. Judgements are not lasting, and your mind can generally change, so don't get excessively made up for lost time in your underlying judgements of anything.

7. Return to the present moment.

On the off chance that you start to feel anxious about the future or remorseful about the past, return your attention to the current moment. Stop and acknowledge there is nothing you can do to transform whatever has just occurred or anything that might be coming to you later on. Continuously come back to the present time and place to live in peace.

8. Try not to be excessively hard on yourself.

when your mind strays during training. Carefully take your thoughts back to the present. Everybody's mind will wander occasionally while they are practicing mindfulness meditation. It is alright to perceive your passing idea and let it go. When it is gone, take some full breaths and reset your focus to be in your mindfulness practice.

9. Connect with your senses.

Your senses; touch, smell, taste, sound and sight - are your passage into the present moment. Be that as it may, when you are somewhere out in dreamland, you don't encounter what your senses are grabbing. Pause to absorb the wonderful smell of your coffee. The salty sea air. The beauty and decent variety of flowers in your neighborhood. The mouth-watering float of wood-fire pizza coming from your nearby Italian eatery as you pass it.

Notice how your dress feels against your body. The delicate clean bed sheets on your skin in the first part of the day. The soothing warmth of your darling's kiss. The grass under your feet. The impression of water and suds on your hands as you do the cleaning up.

Put love and attention into the simple tasks of your day, and you will be stunned how much satisfaction and peace they can bring you.

10. Pause between activity.

Pause and listen to the sound of the telephone ringing before answering it. Pause and feel the heaviness of your body in your seat before starting your work for the afternoon.
Pause and feel the entryway handle of your home before you open it toward the day's end.

Placing smaller than expected pause between activities in your day can ground you in your inward being, clear your mind, and furnish you with fresh energy for the new assignment ahead.

Consider it like putting energetic bookends toward the beginning and end of every movement.

6. Listen wholeheartedly.

The vast majority of us never really listen to individuals when they are addressing us, since we're too bustling arranging what to state next, making a judgment about what they are stating, or becoming mixed up in daydreams altogether.

Next time you're in a discussion, make it your objective to completely listen to what the other individual is stating to you, without losing all sense of direction in your thoughts.

Trust that you will intuitvely realize the best thing to state next when it's your go to talk.

7. Get lost in the flow of accomplishing things you love. We as a whole have certain exercises we love doing ; they interface us with our internal soul and bring us completely alive. For you it could be cooking, singing, dancing, planting, composing, painting, strolling, swimming or building a furniture.

We love accomplishing these things so much that we frequently lose ourselves in them. That is, we lose our littler self - our agitating thoughts and stresses; in light of the fact that we are pouring the majority of our love and attention into the present minute. Include more stream exercises in your week after week schedule, and your happiness will soar.

8. Meditate daily There's no way to avoid it; meditation has enormous advantages and expands your degrees of energy, joy, motivation and inward peace.

It doesn't need to take long. Indeed, even 10 minutes daily can positively affect your life. It will likewise fortify your mindfulness muscles, so you'll see it a lot simpler to wind up present for the duration of the day.

Chapter 3: Intro To Cognitive Restructuring

Mindfulness and cognitive restructuring fit like chutney and cheese. In CBT, mindfulness is typically used together with cognitive restructuring to the point that they are indivisible.

Utilizing mindfulness meditation and mindfulness in awake life is going to assist you in discovering how to step back from your feelings and with time, you'll discover that you end up being calmer, more concentrated and healthier.

But it could be used for a great deal more once you acknowledge the strength this tool has for creating change. The point is that when you recognize negative thoughts that are detrimentally impacting your life, you can now transform them. And that's where cognitive restructuring shows up.

A Short Primer on CBT

CBT is right now the most prominent choice for dealing with mental illness among the majority of big health organizations. The approach was presented fairly recently and is an organic extension of another institution of psychology that reigned previously (around the 50s).

That institution was 'behaviorism' and was completely described by the idea of conditioning and association. The concept was that in case you experienced two stimuli simultaneously frequently enough, they would ultimately end up being linked in your head.

Today we understand this to be correct: in neuroplasticity 'neurons that fire together, wire together'. This implies that if two neurons activate at the same moment frequently enough, they eventually develop a very solid connection which could cause the other to fire unwillingly.

This was shown famously by Ivan Pavlov who practiced with on dogs. He rang a bell any time he fed the canine attendees and gradually, this developed an association by means of 'positive reinforcement'. Eventually, this resulted in the dogs drooling whenever the bell was sounded. As far as their minds were involved, bell equaled food.

This very same idea was after that applied to human psychology. The theory was that we might learn fears, for instance, by associating unfavorable experiences with benign objects. Also, it was supposed that you could manage a fear via 'reassociation.' In case you ensure that someone associates that input with favorable things again, they ultimately lose the fear. And this technique proved effective in various studies.

Behaviorism went a bit too far, it declared that each aspect of the human journey was learned in this manner. We found out how to gesture since when we grabbed things as kids, folks passed them to us. We understood to walk since we kept tipping over when we did it incorrectly Etc.

Whatever we did then was thought to be completely encouraged by the reward centers of our mind, which consequently helped us create fresh associations and establish new behaviors. The things we didn't find out ourselves directly, we could learn 'vicariously' via social conditioning, observing others for instance.

For many years this idea ruled supreme but ultimately, it began to lose favor as it was powerless to clarify every element of our psychology. Eventually, it became evident that there has to be an additional 'interior' aspect and this is where the 'cognitive' part appears. Cognitive behavioral therapy then takes behavioralism and employs the concept that you can also strengthen experiences, both good and bad, by contemplating them.

For example, you can learn to be scared of heights even when you've never slipped from a height. How? By continuously considering how unpleasant it could be to fall from a height. Simply put, if you keep visualizing that falling must be harmful and if you say to yourself things such as 'those railings don't appear safe', then you can induce yourself to be scared.

What's more, is that every time you think something such as this and then avoid the height as a consequence, you are basically strengthening that belief as if you had fallen.

So the concept behind CBT is to utilize the fundamentals of behaviorism but to integrate these with the cognitive element. That implies not only utilizing elements such as 'reassociation' but also 'thinking' cures.

Techniques Used in CBT

So one instance of this is to utilize mindfulness meditation. Just by deciding not to allow your thoughts and feelings impact you, you can end up being less managed by them and consequently less prone to your own worries and ruminations.

But there are a lot more facets to this too and these have a tendency to fall under the heading of 'cognitive restructuring' or simply put-- altering your thoughts.

One instance is a thing called 'thought challenging.' Here, you just break down one of your thoughts or theories and thereby evaluate just how precise it is. For example, you could find that you are scared of speaking in public because you believe people will giggle at you if you stutter. This is a devastating belief that is actually making you far more prone to stuttering.

So what you have to do if you want to conquer this is to look at the notion and ask: is it reasonable? What you'll discover 90% of the time is that this idea is unlikely and misguided. The majority of people would not be cruel enough to make fun of you if you stuttered and even if they did, it wouldn't make a difference since you wouldn't see them again.

Maybe you could feel lame in case you stutter and folks laugh. Once again, you ought to evaluate that: having the ability to chat confidently; however, it comes out and not worry about the result is, in fact, an indication that you're quite self-assured and unconcerned!

I, in fact, utilized this method myself when I had a phobia. I used to come with a somewhat unpleasant phobia of peeing in public urinals. My worry was that if I couldn't go, at that point individuals would look at me and assume I was unusual for mingling there and 'not actually doing anything.'

Then I recognized that the majority of the time I was in that scenario, I was in the bar. Simply put? The majority of the other people in the toilets were most likely drunk and unaware of what I was doing! On the other hand, why did it matter what they believed anyway? Allow them to believe that! Ultimately, this helped me to conquer the phobia entirely, and now I have no issue whatsoever with it.

Another instance is one that combines the suggestions from CBT with more conventional ideas from behaviorism. This one is called 'hypothesis testing.' Basically, it implies that you're evaluating your theory to figure out if it truly holds up.

So if you're scared folks will laugh if you stutter throughout public speaking, that implies you need to stutter on stage and allow everybody to see it intentionally. This will then consequently show you what occurs in that situation and what you'll probably discover is that nothing at all happens. Individuals are kind and they'll simply await you to wrap up and begin again.

Once more, I employed this in the real world. Except I really had no say in it this time. I was learning to drive and I kept delaying any time the lights turned green and I was at the front. Naturally, this occurred because of nerves: I was concerned that if I didn't leave faster off the mark, at that point, the traffic behind me would get upset and it would be extremely awkward.

So my driving instructor, being sort of a rebel, chose to slam on my handbrake and told me that we were going to sit there for the whole time that the light was green. Traffic behind me beeped their horns, people yelled, but not a thing occurred.

Chapter 4: Meditation Can Help You Achieve Your Goal

Essentially, in any case if there are bunches of Meditation Techniques for Beginners, they all have one normal objective and that is to center the brain on a more solid condition of being.

You can accomplish those through different routines yet Meditation for Beginners is truly straightforward. The main affection individuals present why they don't give it a go is on the grounds that they have a troublesome time concentrating. They say that their brains meander off.

This plan can, point of fact, give help with that. It includes joining mindful breathing and origination, things which everybody has the capacity do.

One of the finest methods to "relieve the psyche" is to make your breathing example the point of convergence of your consideration. When you close your eyes and center your regard for your breathing, you can hope to feel your contemplations starting to unwind. Utilizing your nose to breathe in and your mouth to breathe out is the best strategy of doing this.

It's terribly basic to the body that you inhale profoundly. The all the more seriously you inhale, the slower the pace of your pulse. Your body will unwind much more when the measure of oxygen transported to the mind increments and this is a physiological actuality.

It's very discernible that despite the fact that there are diverse Meditation Techniques for Beginners, they all go around a fundamental subject: focusing in on your breath. When you begin having control once again your breathing, then you'll have complete control over your level of anxiety too.

A basic and crucial method incorporated in Meditation for Beginners is perception which happens to be an exceptionally compelling instrument. Science has demonstrated that the mind is crippled to distinguish the distinction between envisioning an activity and truly acting it out. Henceforth in both cases, the cerebrum creates a synthetic that is as what makes the muscles work similarly. Whether the body really does something or not is totally insignificant.

This implies something colossal. Overall, its letting us know that envisioning something has a broad impact on your body. When you get to be capable at consoling your brain through your breathing example, you may incorporate view of the majority of the stuff you wish to have paying little heed to whether its a thing or an inclination.

In case you're examining How to Meditate in light of the fact that you yearning to achieve an easy condition of rest, then you can absolutely imagine things that imply unwinding for you. You can really invoke pictures of the woods, the ocean or anyone of water. You may additionally envision something you can't touch like shafts of hued light, an image or example, or whatever else that puts your psyche very still.

After you get to be capable in Meditation Techniques for Beginners, you may expand your routine by incorporating unwinding music alongside different things identified with reflection. The imperative thing here is to never surrender however rather make contemplation a practice that you basically incorporate inside of your day by day schedule.

Still, never consider contemplation as a commitment. Try not to overlook your body. On the off chance that you don't think you could ruminate, there's dependably a next time. Consider that very much executed reflection that keeps going 10 minutes is constantly better than contemplation finished with an overwhelming heart. Quality as opposed to amount is what's fundamental in reflection.

Chapter 5: Overcoming Negative Thoughts Mindfully

Once we take note of our thoughts and know where they are taking us, we will be in a position to change our relation with them. Our thoughts will determine how our day will unfold, and how we will handle any challenges we encounter during the day. Negative thoughts will cause stress afterwards. This means that to avoid stress, you have to deal with negative thoughts.

The following are ways to overcome negative thoughts mindfully:

Identify the thought- The first step is for you to recognize that some negative thoughts are building up in your mind. The thoughts will be discouraging, such as you can't make it in life, you are not good to handle a problem etc.

Release your body, Release the thoughts- Once you experience negative thoughts, the body will begin to react. Since it is a form of fight, the best thing for you to do is to relax your body. Mindful breathing will also help you release tension from your body through an outward breath. This will also do away with any negative thought which flows through your mind.

Change your thoughts- Now that you can overcome the negative thought, it is time for you to determine what is positive for you. Think about the nice job that you have and feel thankful about it. Think about the good friends you have who will never leave in times of trouble. Think about the wonderful family that you have. Think about the body you have in a well-functioning state. Just identify anything positive about you and try to be thankful about it.

Practice yoga- Try to do the hard yoga poses. Through yoga, one will focus on the present as we will be more after the changes which are made in our body.

Research has shown that maintaining a challenging pose and breathing in and out will help divert attention from your problem to that pose. This is as a result of the discomfort you will feel in a pose. During times of stress, one thinks that the problem will never end. However, by practicing yoga, the most challenging pose helps us accept the problem, and trust the future for a better outcome.

Think about the children and animal life- Children and animals are more concentrated about what is at the present and they act according to it. A dog will never think about the look it got from a neighbor the previous day. Seek for ways on how to bring some small curiosity in your life, in the same way children and dogs do it. This will make us not look for ways on how to push our thoughts or get attached to them. The best thing is to explore such thoughts in the same way that children do, and we will see them as just thoughts.

Practice mindful listening- When listening mindfully, your attention should just be focused towards listening. Allow the speaker to express his or her views, and do not respond in any way just listen. You should not agree, disagree or interrupt in any way. This practice of mindful listening is also a good show of respect to the speaker and you will understand his or her message deeply.

Shower mindfully- The most basic activities which are done on a daily basis are usually done mindlessly. However, such activities are very good for us to practice mindfulness. When you shower, focus on how the water feels on your skin. Feel the temperature of the water. Enjoy the scent of the shampoo, and the pressure of the water. Try to bring yourself to that moment and focus on what you are doing, and this will help you overcome stress.

Chapter 6: Mindfulness Exercises For Beginners

After sitting down, settling in, and cultivating the right attitudes towards meditation, it is now time to enter the state of mindfulness. This chapter discusses four exercises you can perform to achieve mindfulness meditation.

Mindful Breathing

You may wish to focus on mindfully counting your breaths at the moment. In this exercise, you do not think of the future anymore, nor think of the past. You do not think of your unfinished errands or past heartaches, because you are placing your full attention on the present moment, specifically on your breathing.

Start by taking three deep breaths. Breathe normally afterwards. Focus on the rims of your nostrils and let your breathing effortlessly flow in and out. Try to distinguish the parts of your breaths, including the brief pause in between finishing an inhalation and before beginning an exhalation. After exhalation, notice another brief pause before inhaling begins. The two pauses happen in such a brief moment that you are normally not aware of them. When you are mindful, however, you can fully appreciate them.

At the start of this exercise, you will have short inhalations and exhalations since your body and mind are not yet relaxed. Notice the feeling of that short inhalation and short exhalation as they occur. While doing this, your body and mind will eventually calm down and your breath lengthens and becomes subtle. Notice this peaceful and relaxing feeling of your breathing.

Concentration

In this exercise, you follow your in-breath from start to the end. Do this for your out-breath as well. If your in-breath is three or four seconds long, then your mindfulness will also be that long. Keep your focus on your breathing all throughout as air flows in and out of your body. In this way, mindfulness is uninterrupted and your awareness is sustained. This improves the quality of your concentration.

When you are breathing in, and then suddenly you remember, "Oh, I forgot to turn off the TV in the other room," then there is interruption in your concentration. Just stick to breathing all the way through so you become your in-breath and your out-breath. Continuing this will naturally make your breathing deeper, slower, more peaceful and harmonious.

Body Awareness

This exercise takes mindful breathing one step further. It is by becoming conscious of your entire body while you are breathing. "As I breathe in, I am conscious of my body. As I breathe out, I am conscious of my body." In the first exercise, you become conscious of your in-breath and out-breath. Since you now have created the energy of mindfulness by breathing, you can use that force to recognize your body and be fully aware that it is in this particular moment and space.

Releasing Tension

This exercise releases accumulated tension, emotions, or pain in your body. When stresses build up inside you for a long time, the body suffers. The mind is not there to assist its release. Release tension by visiting each part of the body. Start, for example, with the right foot and work up to towards the top of your head. The aim is simply to be aware of whatever sensations (e.g. temperature, touch of clothing, pulse, current of energy, etc.) you are experiencing at every part of your body. Any relaxation that may be felt should be considered as just a by-product. Paradoxically, the more you consider mindfulness as a pure awareness exercise—without thinking or hoping for benefits—the more you improve your well-being.

Chapter 7: Mindfulness Meditation In Depth

Why do people do mindfulness meditation? The reasons may not be clear to you at first, but it is worthwhile noting the scientific facts surrounding Mindfulness Meditation. Before we give you the step by step instructions, you need to know why it helps and who it helps.

How Meditation helps with depression relief

Meditation is used to help people who are depressed because it helps them to focus their attention on something other than negativity. When people are depressed, they tend to go over the same negative thoughts and go back to times when they have been hurt by life. Depression is an accumulation of different emotional responses to a stimuli, but not everyone reacts in the same way. There are patterns of behavior that tend to push people toward depression. By learning to meditate and to involve yourself in mindfulness, you learn ways to accept yourself and to understand the workings of the inner mind better, so that you don't have to dwell on the negative.

Scientists who did research on the brains of people who regularly meditated found that there was more activity in areas of the brain that meant better efficiency in the memory, as well as a much more peaceful demeanor. They were not prone to depression and certainly displayed a kind of oneness, which was not present in the scan of someone who did not meditate. They were calmer and more focused which generally meant that they were more contented. There are obvious benefits for those who are depressed because often their thought patterns are negative and, as such, will encourage even more negative thought. If you take away those negative thoughts and replace them with breathing exercises such as are done when people meditate, it becomes easier for depressed people to find peace. This practice also lowers blood pressure and heart rate, which may be too high caused by depression.

While it may be harder at first for those suffering from depression, after a while the benefits outweigh the inconvenience. You start to learn to let go of negative thoughts and replace them with thoughts about the moment that you are in. This helps you to train your mind toward the positive, rather than grasping hold of the negative and believing there is no alternative. This is one of the reasons that mindfulness meditation is being recommended by general practitioners for people suffering from chronic or repeated depression, as an alternative to traditional medicines. In the United Kingdom this has proven to be a popular choice and a successful one at that. The frontal cortex, which is responsible for wellbeing and happiness, shows decreased activity while someone is depressed. However, this is the area targeted by mindfulness meditation and changes have been noted that are positive and that mean that subjects are less prone to depression and more drawn toward seeking solutions of a positive nature.

How Meditation helps with anxiety relief

Mindfulness meditation helps the sufferer to slow down in the breathing techniques used. This in turn stops the body from producing too much oxygen and over-oxygenating the system. In fact, half of the feeling of anxiety is as a result of panic and over-oxygenation and breathing correctly can normalize this. You may have heard of people being asked to breathe into a paper bag when they feel anxious. Meditation does the same thing in that you inhale much deeper than normal and exhale as shown in the instructions for mindful meditation later in this book. This makes the stress less hard to cope with and the anxiety lessens when you are able to look at the problems in question with a clear mind. Quite often anxiety is as a direct result of over-thinking things and mindfulness helps you to base your thoughts in the moment, rather than holding onto them and trying to deal with things en-masse. When the mind is in overload, stresses occur. Thus, mindfulness slows down that process and allows an individual to be able to cope in a more effective way.

How Meditation can help with pain

Pain management experts are using meditation to help patients to deal with chronic pain. The reason that it helps is that it relaxes the body and mind and the concentration on the area of pain. When this is all that you have focus on, then of course, the pain comes before everything else, but when you learn to meditate, you take your mind away from thinking about the pain, while still being aware of it, and not judging it in any way except that it may be a slight irritation. Gabriel Tan, a pain psychologist from Houston said in a report on pain that you cannot actually experience pain unless your thoughts are centered upon it. Therefore, giving the mind something else to concentrate on takes the emphasis off the pain and thus makes it easier for people with painful conditions to get through those bad times when the pain seems to be unbearable. Studies from Switzerland back this up and say that meditation helps chronic sufferers of illnesses like fibromyalgia to cope with pain and to deal with the depression that comes with the illness. In fact in a follow through three years later, those patients who had chosen to practice mindful meditation were still able to cope with their painful symptoms and found improvement in their state of mind. The only difference between treating people who are mobile and those who were less mobile was that it helped to teach lying down relaxation methods that lead to meditation, as this seemed to be easier on their bodies.

How Meditation can help with stress

We know that people who are stressed suffer from increased blood pressure, quicker heartbeat and exaggerated breathing. What this does inside the body is release a hormone called cortisol. Cortisol in small doses is reasonable, but when you system overloads, it has consequences. These include health threats and anxiety, depression and even heart problems and thus meditation is used to calm down the breathing and to regulate the production of this cortisol. In excess, it can make you feel very ill indeed and this adds to the stress factor. Let me give you an example. A young woman worries because she feels pains in her chest. She is alone and she is afraid. This makes her even more stressed. The body's answer to this stress is the release of cortisol. This adds to the stress, makes the heart beat faster and makes the blood pressure even higher. Instead of helping her, it hinders her thought processes in that she will concentrate on the pain, logically trying to find a solution for it although thinking the worst. This kind of stress is common in this day and age, but meditation does so much for you that it isn't simply a case of bringing down your blood pressure. It opens up avenues for creativity, as scientists have seen on the MRIs of practicing Buddhist monks and your awareness of self. This awareness also helps you to understand what's going on in your body and be able to listen to it in a more effective way, thus cutting down the stress and the cortisol at the same time.

When a company asked its employees to take part in Meditation and this was measured over a period of time, what they found was that stress was reduced by 28 percent, 20 percent of the employees suffered less pain and consequently needed less time off work and 19 percent of the people involved found as a side effect to meditation that they actually got a good night's sleep. That's amazing news for those starting out on the journey into meditation, because it's not a hard thing to do, but it can make all the difference in the world to how you greet the world and how your body reacts to the lifestyle that you are living. Getting sufficient sleep is vital, because this allows the natural healing processes of the body to function. Getting up and then meditating starts the day on a positive note and helps people who are easily stressed to reduce that stress to a minimum.

How Meditation helps with illness in general

When you meditate on a regular basis you are more in touch with the way that your body feels and are aware of changes that need you to introduce changes in habit. The relationship between you and your inner self is improved and you are unlikely to abuse your body knowing that the habits you have been following are causing illness to occur. Drinking more water and exercising on a regular basis are part of life but part that many neglect. However, when you meditate, you have a crystal clear idea of what your body needs in order to recuperate. You tend not to neglect yourself and understand that personal suffering is simply your body sending a message to your brain to help you to understand yourself better. People who are busy in their stressed lives and who do not meditate don't find the time to deal with small ailments and these then become long term ailments, whereas someone who meditates is instantly aware of small things and deals with them. The spiritual part of the equation is important as well because people who practice mindfulness are aware of their senses and know that they are more than the sum of their discomfort. When the discomfort of illness is dealt with in a timely manner, they suffer less and it makes perfect sense to them that their senses are guiding them to better look after themselves.

You can see from this chapter, that there's a lot on information to get your head around, but once you start to meditate, you also find that all of the benefits become very real. I have devoted the next chapter to the benefits of mindful meditation because the benefits go far and wide beyond illness. From the next chapter, you will be able to see how mindful meditation makes you feel and why you feel that way. It is merely a question of getting in tune with your own mind and that's what the world today does not really give you the opportunity to do. We are too busy in our lives and people are starting to realize that you cannot judge your life by what you own, nor your success by what position you hold within a company. If your thoughts and feelings are muddled, then being rich or being successful won't change that muddle although meditation can.

How Meditation helps with concentration

The John Moore University in Liverpool studied the effects of meditation for a simple period of 20 minutes a day on the levels of concentration of students as opposed to those students who did not perform meditation. During the 16 week study, in which 40 adults took part, tests were given that allowed the scientists to measure the level of concentration and this clearly showed that those who meditated were better able and equipped to answer the questions asked of them.

As you will find in a later chapter, concentration is sharper and more focused when practicing mindfulness meditation on a regular basis. Imagine the mind as a series of cardboard boxes. Every time that the mind is drawn toward one of these boxes or another, it evokes emotions. These remain open in the mind that does not practice meditation, while in those who do, the mind is more organized and less likely to succumb to forgetfulness. The focus is sharper, as if the weight of those boxes of thoughts has been taken away and the mind is left to concentrate on what is particularly important at that moment in time.

It's also worth noting that even small breathing exercises used at points during the day can help the clarity of the mind and the perception of the practitioner.

How Meditation helps self-acceptance

Mindfulness meditation allows you to spend more time exclusively with yourself and you get to know yourself better than you would normally do. Friendliness and kindness are part of the picture as well as empathy and understanding. When you have practiced mindfulness meditation, you have a better mental picture of who you are rather than who people say you are. The compassion that you feel from mindfulness meditation helps you to accept yourself and to be kinder to the person you are. Negative thoughts are not encouraged, but they are acknowledged. You can't hide them because they will happen, but students are taught how to deal with them and how to give them less importance. Thus, individuals become mentally stronger and able to see these negative aspects of their thinking for what they are. Meditation teaches you to let go, but to be aware of those thoughts and when you self-correct your own way of thinking because you have become aware of it during meditation, you become more humble in your approach to life and less expectant of praise from others. Don't expect things to change overnight. You need to learn a new approach and that's exactly what mindfulness meditation is. It's not about avoiding criticism of self. It's about accepting self, even though there may be negativities that need to be straightened out. It's all part of who you are in this moment in time. Meditation helps you to improve that self and thus works on your self-esteem and self-acceptance, but not to the extent that you become superior. The mistake that people make is expecting the world to change without actually having put in the effort, but when you know that the effort is so little, it's hard to fight the facts that are presented in this book and backed up by scientists, that the habit of mindfulness allows you to live a happier life and to get to know yourself better and to love yourself more without believing that you have all of the answers to life's dilemmas.

The reason that you need to work on your self-esteem is that over the course of your life, you are influenced by the things that people say to you and the feedback that you get from people all of your life. These people may be parents or siblings, they may be peers. The fact is that everyone goes through this stage of having feedback and some come out of it worse off than others. When you meditate and learn to breathe correctly, you start to see yourself as a stronger person and your brain is in fact processing things in a different way. The fight or flight that you experience when you are afraid is, to a certain extent diminished and you feel a sense of wellbeing. Within that sense of wellbeing, you also learn that this moment is who you are. The mistakes of the past are not here anymore and what you do from this moment onward makes a difference to how you see yourself and develop yourself into a human being capable of great love and compassion.

Many people believe that meditating means emptying the mind and that's where the thought is erroneous. It is a case of filling the mind with relevance and understanding what's going on inside it that helps you to correct the way that you look at life and the way that others look at you within that life. Mindfulness meditation on a daily basis will actually change the structure of your brain so that you think in a different way and become happy with the person you present to the world, no matter how hard your background was, or how much you feel that you have suffered in your life. Not only that, but it will strengthen your character so that in the future, you are able to deal with the blows of life with a much more philosophical response that strengthens you rather than weakens who you are.

These are all of the ways that mindfulness meditation can help. There are probably more, but for the time being I have dealt with the suffering of the mind and how it helps to balance out your thoughts so that you are able to get beyond depression, anxiety, self-esteem issues and all of the negative things you may have been experiencing up until this point in time. It does require commitment, so when you start the meditation process, be sure that you are ready to embrace this new way of looking at life so that you gain maximum benefit from it, rather than giving it a half-hearted attempt and then giving up.

Chapter 8: The Practice Of Mindfulness And Meditation.

These are tools to help you in the cultivation of mindfulness, both as a formal meditation practice and in your everyday life. Remember the benefits of these practices not only heal you spiritually but physically as well.

Mindfulness can be defined as the awareness that comes from living and focusing on the present moment at any given time.

It is your wholesome awareness of being alive and experiencing feelings deep within you as well as those bombarding your physical body simultaneously.

This acute awareness allows you to pinpoint focus on problems, areas in your life that need balance, and spiritual renewal and understanding that you do have a true purpose.

The reason people suddenly manage to solve their problems using mindfulness and meditation techniques is because of the new understanding and awareness they have of them.

Instead of fighting these problems that awareness provides you with solutions you would not have thought of otherwise. These are no longer barriers in your existence.

Mindfulness creates wisdom, understanding of your inner strengths, and your link to others, your purpose and your destiny.

Sure all of this certainly does sound like a lot of religious hocus pocus...

However, scientific studies have even proven healing for diseases and even in the media it has been recently mentioned that mindfulness training is a better form of treatment for depression than a course of anti depressant medication.

Meditation enhances deep relaxation while practicing mindfulness, and combined with proper forms of Yoga the benefits are numerous.

During deep transcendental meditation mindfulness practices well being cocoons you for everything around you, even if you have been facing stressful situations, difficult problems and even pain and illness.

"It's All About Uncovering Your Self and Purpose in Life."

Finding out what is best for yourself in every area of your life will be revealed through mindfulness and meditation techniques.

Once you have mastered mind control through mindfulness practices, you can map your life into fulfillment choosing for tranquility, peace and harmony even though the world around you is swirling with fast paced technologies and noise.

After a tough day at work and for busy lifestyles nothing is more calming than listening to the sounds of nature.

However you don't need to wait for the end of the day to practice calming relaxation meditation because once you have mastered the art then you will feel refreshed with short periods of meditation anytime and anywhere during your busy lifestyle!

Chapter 9: Techniques And Practice

There are several techniques that you can employ in your life to help you to become more mindful. The body scan is one particular way that helps you to stay in the moment but be very conscious about your body.

The Body Scan

This is a technique that is used to help you to feel relaxed and happy in the skin you are in. I would suggest that you lie down on your bed for this exercise. You are going to be thinking about the different parts of your body and while you are doing this, need to be aware of thoughts that try and impose themselves upon you. When thoughts come that are not related to the body scan, you simply observe them, acknowledge them and then let them go, without allowing them to penetrate deeper consciousness.

Start with your toes. Think of your toes. Think about how they feel. Think about the way that your socks feel against your toes. Feel your toes tense up and then relax.

You go through all the different parts of the body and the only thoughts that you should have while you do this is the part of the body in question. If you feel some discomfort, you simply observe it but do nothing about it. "I have a twitch in my arm" is an observation. However, you don't need to delve deeper to try and find out why you have a twitch in your arm. The practice is simply going through all of the body parts, tensing them up and relaxing them, examining how they feel but placing no judgment or logic on how they feel.

By the end of the body scan you will find that your blood pressure and heart rate will have gone down and you will be completely relaxed. Thus, take your time to get up from this position to allow your body to adjust.

The self-love challenge

People often live their lives with negative thoughts about who they are. For the self-love challenge, you need to let go of those thoughts and start to concentrate on things that are good about you. You can improve on all kinds of areas in your life that help you to feel better about yourself and should note these down in your journal and learn to feel that you are giving yourself the credit for being the best person that you can be. Often when you talk about self-love people think it a little strange. However, unless you do have a certain amount of love for yourself, how can you expect people around you to love you? Therefore it's central to all of your relationships in life. It's not egoism and it's not putting your own needs first. It's just about appreciating who you are in this moment in time. Here are some challenges that you can give yourself daily to improve your love for yourself:

- Smile at people around you and note the response

- Let go of angry feelings by using mindfulness breathing

- Let go of stress by doing the body scan

- Do your daily meditation

- Learn to be consciously in the moment at all times that you can during the day

- Use your ability to stay in the moment to help your focus on work

- Use your ability to stay in the moment to listen to others

- Use this moment to do something kind for someone else

All of these actions help you to appreciate your life more. They also help you to become mindful without judgment of others. Learning to stop being judgmental is one of the most fundamental lessons of mindfulness and it is something that you need to practice because for years, you will have judged because that's what society encouraged you to do. Note down the times you were able to skip judgment and help someone who needed your help.

Learn to foster friendships that are two way and give equally as much to the moments you spend with friends as they do.

Mindfulness is a way of life. It's a very valuable one and once you understand it, then chances of stepping back from that way of life are less likely. It's a more satisfying way to be and when you live in the moment, your appreciation of life soars. Enjoy the calm of being alone. Enjoy the cobwebs on the bushes in the garden in the early morning as the dewdrops hang like diamonds. Be in the moment, be in the now, and love yourself and your life because that's when life changes for the better.

Creativity

It is important that you have a level of creativity in your life. Whether this is making model planes or flower arranging, try to incorporate something that allows your creative juices to flow. This will help you to balance out the use of the two hemispheres of the brain, which is very useful for people who practice meditation. Drawing, doodling, coloring in are all crafts that you can enjoy and that focus the mind on one particular thing which will help you to use your mindfulness mode for longer periods of time. This helps you to cut down the stress levels in your life.

Learning and Exercising the Brain

Do things like enjoying a crossword in the paper or playing backgammon or other games with family and friends. These help the logical side of the brain to work. It also increases your awareness of the world around you. Enjoy reading books and make these part of your mindfulness practice. The better the book, the more you get absorbed into the characters and the scenarios and this really does help you to keep your mind on the moment that you are in.

If you try some of these exercises, you will find that they really do hone your instincts and help you to incorporate mindfulness into your life. One of the best exercises for the senses was introduced to me by my children. If you place certain objects into pairs of Wellington boots, such as grains of rice, pasta pieces or different textures, you can use this to help you to use the sense of touch to decide what they are. It's a great party game and all of the family can enjoy being in the moment and using their senses to try and win.

Chapter 10: Body Scan Meditation

When you experience chronic stress that triggers stimuli in your body, you may feel numbness, pain or discomfort in some parts of your body. Stress, anxiety and even sitting for long periods of time at the office lead to this unpleasant sensation in your body. To overcome this feeling, you should practice another technique called body scan mindfulness meditation.

What Is Body Scan Meditation?

Body scan meditation is a technique done by analyzing how and what your body feels rather than paying attention to the thoughts about what your body feels. When stressful thoughts rule your mind, your body becomes stressed too.

Body parts such as your shoulders, stomach and back feel tensed when you are highly upset and that's because stress directly affects your body. Body scan meditation effectively helps you get rid of the stress stuck in your body; and it helps you become more mindful of your body too.

Follow this step-by-step guide to practice body scan mindfulness meditation.

Practicing Body Scan Meditation

Start by lying on your back in a comfortable position. Make sure that your posture makes you feel relaxed. If you are feeling pain in your back by lying on it then adjust your position to feel comfortable. You can slide a pillow under your back to avoid pain or even lie on your side if lying on your back is too painful.

As soon as you settle, start breathing deeply and focus on your breath for a few minutes to calm down your racing mind.

Slowly shift your attention from your breath to your body. Start feeling the tingling sensation in your toes and the different sensations you feel in your feet.

Shift your attention from toes to the other parts of your body. Feel each part of your body at a time as you move up from your toes to your head. Focus intensely on the sensation or tension in every part.

If at any time, your mind gets back to your thoughts, drag it back to your body by feeling the sensations such as pain in your back or burning sensation in your stomach.

Do this exercise for 20-30 minutes or even for 10 minutes in the beginning if you are a beginner. You will need to be patient to get to the point of being able to practice the technique without being distracted. Keep fighting your mind by focusing back on your body if your mind starts thinking about stressful thoughts. Feel each sensation in your body as it happens.

Practice body scan meditation on a regular basis. You can write down the sensation you felt in each part of your body. It makes you more mindful of your body; and the next time you practice body scan meditation, you will pay more attention to your body than to your mind. For instance, if you felt tension in your calves then write it down. In the next practice session, your focus will be more when you feel your calves.

Your quest to become completely mindful doesn't end here. To become completely mindful, you can incorporate mindfulness to your daily routine, which I'll discuss in the next chapter.

Chapter 11: Simple Tips For Being More Mindful Everyday

Mindfulness is all about tuning the brain to focus on the present moment. It is important to state this fact because sometimes the true essence of mindfulness is lost. This happens when putting all emphasis on traditional activities practiced alongside mindfulness such as meditation or yoga. However, mindfulness can be applied in our daily lives.

By focusing on the here and now, this gives us greater peace of mind and clarity.Using this approach, we can avoid drifting through our lives in confusion, being consumed by thoughts of what could have been or planning for things that are out of our control.

There are many simple ways to practice mindfulness on a daily basis;

Mindful Eating

Eating mindfully is something that many people take for granted. All too often, many of us are always in a hurry to finish a meal only to miss enjoying one of life's most simple and wonderful pleasures. Next time when having a meal, try to eat mindfully. Before you begin eating, take notice of the presentation of food and the scent. Remember to take small bites and chew slowly while paying attention to the texture and taste of the food. When you immerse yourself fully in the moment, this not only makes mindful eating more enjoyable, but also helps with digestion and prevents overeating.

Listen Mindfully

Conversations with other people present another great opportunity to put active mindfulness into practice. Sometimes when other people talk to us, we may be there physically but not with our whole being. We think what to say next or judge what others are saying, mentally agreeing or disagreeing with them before they even finish talking. To listen with mindfulness, you will need to focus fully on others when having a chat. Next time you have a conversation with a loved one or colleague, avoid getting caught up in your own mental chatter. Pay attention to what they are saying. People appreciate when you truly listen and they will likely respond in kind when it is your turn to speak.

Pay More Attention While Attending to One Thing at a Time

In today's fast paced world, multitasking has become a common trend as people attempt to get more done within a short amount of time. And, while people think that multitasking makes us more productive, it only leads to needless quick exhaustion. When one tires quickly, mistakes are bound to be made. This can be avoided by doing things one at a time and with mindfulness. When you take on tasks with full focus, one by one, this leaves little room for mistakes or forgetting things due to rushing. You will find that you are more efficient and less worn out when attending to each task one at time mindfully.

Keep in mind that there are plenty of other opportunities in our daily lives to be mindful and live fully in the moment. By practicing mindfulness on a daily basis, the brain eventually learns how to be more efficient and better integrated. You will start to experience improved focus and less distractibility. Stress levels will go down as well. This in turn will make your daily activities, thoughts, attitudes, and perceptions more balanced.

FREQUENTLY ASKED QUESTIONS ABOUT MINDFULNESS

Is mindfulness the same as meditation?

Mindfulness meditation is one way to practice mindfulness, but since being mindful simply involves paying attention to the present moment, mindfulness can be brought to anything you do. Becoming more mindful takes practice, and mindfulness meditation is good tool to learn to be more mindful. However, you can become more mindful without meditation, and even if you do practice mindfulness meditation, the benefits of mindfulness are greatest when mindfulness is incorporated into everyday life. Many people never practice meditation and find other ways to bring mindfulness into their lives.

Is mindfulness Buddhism?

Mindfulness and mindfulness meditation are an important part of many Buddhist traditions, but there is nothing exclusively Buddhist about mindfulness. Many other religious and spiritual practices involve mindfulness, and you can learn mindfulness and realize its benefits regardless of your religious or spiritual beliefs.

Can anyone learn to be more mindful?

Many people try meditation and find it impossible to keep their mind from wandering and believe that becoming more mindfull is something they will never be able to do. But becoming more mindful does not need to involve meditation, and mindfulness does not involve emptying your mind. Mindfulness simply involves paying attention to whatever is going on in the present moment and learning to bring your mind back to the present whenever you notice it wandering. Mindfulness does not need to involve extended periods of meditation. It can be practiced for just a few minutes at a time, and brought to whatever you are doing in your everyday life. Even if you may never be inclined to meditate, you can still learn to incorporate mindfulness into your life and realize its benefits.

How do I practice mindfulness?

Since mindfulness simply involves paying attention to whatever is going on in the present moment, you can bring mindfulness to any aspect of your life. The formal way to practice mindfulness is through meditation, which involves paying attention to things such as your breath, physical sensations, your thoughts and your emotions. Mindfulness can also be practiced informally by focusing your attention on your breathing for brief periods throughout your day, or by becoming more mindful during everyday activities such as walking, driving, eating, cleaning, or whatever else you may be doing at any given time. As you become more comfortable with being mindful, you will be able to bring mindfulness to your thoughts, your feelings and emotions, and any problems or difficulties you face.

Chapter 12: Gain Understanding And Self-Awareness

Many of us remain only partial aware of the truth of who we are, of what we understand about ourselves, and of what ultimately drives us. Unlocking that understanding within yourself is the ultimate purpose of self-knowledge, and the personal insights that come from attaining self-knowledge are of great value. You will be able to influence both your actions, and your reactions, whether voluntary or involuntary. The process of understanding yourself is a slow and sometimes difficult task, but many will find that self-knowledge is its own reward.

What is the purpose of gaining self-knowledge?

Self-knowledge evades many people, but for those who pursue it, the benefits are endless. For example, though almost all people experience emotion, few are able to truly process and understand an emotion's significance. Mindfulness of emotions allows a person to accept or process emotional responses, instead of allowing emotion to consume, control, or confuse them.

Carrying an internal understanding of yourself allows you to stay calm in frustrating situations, leading to a healthier, simpler resolution of internal and external conflict. There will be no need to turn to vice, including drugs and alcohol. Rather, you will find that difficult and trying circumstances are manageable, and you will develop healthy and strong coping mechanisms.

Stepping back from an immediate, reactionary approach to the world around you will allow you to see and understand patterns that may be recurring in your life. Only the clarity brought about by self-knowledge can break negative cycles and get you out of a rut and moving forward.

What is the best practical method for gaining self-knowledge?

There are many techniques that lead to self-knowledge, but one of the most common methods is called mindfulness of thought. These sessions are a bit more time consuming than other self-knowledge techniques, because each thought requires time and careful observation. You must examine many thoughts, and internalize them so that they can be further processed throughout the day. These sessions can last as longer than 20 minutes, but can be as fast as 10-15 minutes for the well-practiced.

As with any self-knowledge exercise, you must begin with a comfortable meditative position without any external distractions. This allows you to move internally. Begin by becoming mindful of your breathing, and after you have closed yourself off to the world around you, turn your consciousness inward, forgetting the physical act of breathing.

Become mindful of your internal stressors, and allow your thoughts to direct themselves. If you feel peace, allow that feeling to move within you. Do not try to control your thoughts, or change them in any way. Simply observe the direction of your mind, allow yourself to wander, and listen to the natural direction of your mind.

Do not be tempted to reign in your thoughts, always stay disconnected and passive. Make no comments to yourself, and do not begrudge your thoughts. Mindfulness is not a conversational or judgmental process. Allow even your darkest thoughts to flow freely, your cruel and sad impulses. Later, you will be able to reflect on what these thoughts mean, but how will you learn these things if you repress them instead of observing?

After a period of observation, you will naturally begin to shift the direction of your thoughts. At that point, it is time to conclude the session. Before returning to a wakeful state, become once again aware of your breathing. Even after you open your eyes, take a moment to sit and rest. Reflect, or write about your session, and take some time to calm your mind. It is always helpful to write down thoughts that you want to more fully understand, even if you feel calm and collected.

How does mindfulness of thought help attain self-knowledge?

The internal, often unconscious thoughts that you experience in these sessions will allow you to better approach that which you encounter in your external circumstances. You will discover important thought patterns, and for those who find themselves lingering on or harboring darker thoughts, you may discover that you are expending a lot of unconscious effort in keeping those thoughts repressed. Determining the relationships between your innermost thoughts and external reality can lead to acceptance of challenging stressors, new and healthier coping mechanisms, and an overall improvement in your daily life.

What time of day is best to practice mindfulness of thought?

The time of day does not particularly affect one's ability to practice mindfulness of thought. That being said, most find that sessions are more productive immediately before or after going to sleep. Early morning sessions in particular can help you feel balanced and centered throughout the day, which has other immediate benefits in the way that you interact with your environment, particularly the people surrounding you.

Chapter 13: Let's Practice

Every time you meditate, you need to start off with a comfortable sitting position without any discomfort whatever. Make sure the body is relaxed, and the head is balanced comfortably on your shoulders. Wear comfortable clothes so that you don't have any distractions whatsoever. You are aiming at not being distracted when you start the process. When it comes to meditation, how your breath is the factor, your mind and body need to be in tune with each other while focusing on your breathing. Breathing helps you to center your focus on something. Studies show that focusing on deep breathing for just a while will change the mood of a person and reduce stress.

For you to enjoy spiritual meditation, you need to take time to understand what it is they go through the paces of the meditation. Here are the steps to successful spiritual meditation:

Get a Quiet Place

Before you go ahead and start meditating, you need to find a place that is comfortable for you. Make sure you avoid places that are noisy or that have a lot of distractions. Instead, go to a quiet place that will allow you to focus on your inner being. Remember that spiritual meditation can make you sleep; it is therefore ideal that you are extra cautious when choosing the position and the environment. Pick a place that you are comfortable in, but not one that will be too relaxing that you drift into sleep. You can sit on a mat or use a chair. Once you are seated comfortably, you can close your eyes and start experiencing the emotions.

Breathing

Breathing is one of the most effective meditation techniques.

You use your breath to come up with an anchor that will bring your attention to the present moment. When done the right way, it will aid you to achieve inner peace.

It is similar to taking breath of fresh air. Starting to just focus on the way you breathe, which will relax the mind and body and then after few minutes of observing and feeling your natural breath take a deep breath-in through the nose whereas counting up to four, feel the air go through to your lungs and let it fill up your stomach. At end of inhalation, grip breath for some moments, and then while still relaxed, let the air slowly go out through the nose on the exhalation and repeat few times just like that for about four rounds and then slowly come back into your natural breath.

Experience the Process

Now that you have found the right position to help you meditate and created awareness on your breath the next thing is to let go. Loosen up and then let everything take a natural course. When you meditate, you don't do anything actively; instead, you need to go about everything in a natural manner. You need to be a passive spectator, allowing the process to go ahead on its own. Don't be concerned about what will happen or getting things right let it follow its natural course.

Acknowledge Your Thoughts

The world runs on information, and you are always fed with new data all the time. Due to this, the world is always abuzz with new information that our brain needs to react to. The normal reaction is to see what happens when the information is absorbed, and this way, we let the thoughts to bombard us. The aim of meditation is to leave the thoughts to go away; let the ideas get into your thought process, hut take time to control the urge to react to the various thoughts. Focus on your meditation.

Utter a Prayer

As you sit there and avoid thoughts from taking over your mental capacity, you need to choose prayer and utter it. Say anything that will mean something to you. The prayer can be a phrase or a single word. When you do this, make sure your body remains relaxed and loose, and breath naturally and slowly.

Reflect on Your Progress

Look at yourself after the whole process. Find out how the body feels and be attentive to the breath and thoughts. Stay calm and relax, and then open your eyes and let the effects of meditation sink in. Feel how you become less agitated after the session.

Daily Basis

A few minutes each day will aid you train your mind. All you need to do is to inhale and exhale as you feel the various sensations run through your body. This has various benefits that include lower emotional reaction. You don't have to set aside a specific time of day or place to be aware of the breathing throughout the day. You can do this while sitting, standing, or lying down.

The aim is to make sure you have a healthy emotional life that will help you deal with daily stresses. Numerous studies have shown that when you use meditation, you will do away with stress, and you get to reprogram your brain so that you have a better capacity to manage the stress. However, this only happens when you make meditation your daily practice, and you make it consistent.

Chapter 14: Clear Your Energy

Everything in the world is made up of energy. Just as you would come home from a bonfire smelling like smoke, you will also carry with you the energy of people and interactions that you have encountered during the day. Sometimes it is beneficial to you to carry this energy if the interaction was positive and life-affirming, but if you have encountered negativity or toxicity, it does not serve you well to carry that energy back into your safe space.

If you struggle to believe that the energy of one person can attach itself to another person, be assured that the concept of energy transfer is a scientific one. It is also scientifically proven that every human being has an energy field around them that is unique to them. When experiments are done to test the energy field of a person displaying negative emotions, the results are visibly different from the energy field of a person displaying positive emotions. Therefore, it stands to reason that if negative energy has a unique pattern and energy transfer is real, then negative energy transfer is just as valid a phenomenon.

When you have been ill and you've been laying in bed for a few days or even in hospital and you've been unable to have a proper bath or shower, why does it feel so good when you are eventually able to bath or shower? It is because you have cleared the energy that was clinging to you.

Why Do You Need to Protect Your Energy?

The essence of all energy is that it can only be transferred and never destroyed. On a daily basis, we interact with other people and experience events, all of which have an energy of their own—sometimes positive and sometimes negative. While we may wake up and practice all of the techniques we have learned to ensure that we have left the house in a balanced and mindful state, we are inevitably going to come across energies that do not serve us well. If we do not consciously go about protecting our energy, negative energies will be transferred to us and we will carry them around with us.

These negative energies can affect our state of mind and even our health. We can also end up transferring these energies to other people, which is not fair to them. This is why it is vital that we learn how to protect our energy, and this does not only apply to empaths but to everyone as every being is made up of energy.

If you find yourself in a situation where you are forced to spend long periods of time around negative energy, it may be necessary for you to take time away from the situation in order to restore your energy levels and nurture yourself.

If the negative energy onslaught is happening at your place of work, you may need to consider whether it is time to move on permanently, but this decision should be weighed carefully. There are very few, if any, places of work which will not play host to some form of negative energy at some time. If the atmosphere has become toxic, however, and there is a constant barrage of negativity, it may be time to separate yourself from that.

For workplaces where there is only occasional negativity, you can take a sick day in order to restore yourself. For many, the idea of taking a self-care day from work may seem alien and even result in guilty feelings. If you are one of these people, you should keep in mind that you cannot pour from an empty cup. If you become burned out and exhausted, you will not be able to do your job properly. This may, in severe situations, end up in you being dismissed, which will only worsen your personal situation. Try and see a self-care day as an investment in your overall performance and well-being (Bui, n.d.).

Even the spoken word has an energy. The energy attached to a word emanates from the person speaking the word and will carry the energy that they have spoken into that word from their own perspective.

Animals are highly tuned to energy. You will note that a pack of dogs that may be sleeping or in a state of rest and relaxation around one person but may immediately perk up and start to behave excitedly around another person. The individual may not feel that they are the cause of the excitement, but they are. If they were to really assess and analyze how they are feeling, they will pick up either highly excitable positive emotions or even negative emotions such as fear and nervousness.

Spending time around animals is, therefore, a very good way to practice shifting your energy as they are almost immediate mirrors of the energy you are giving off and it is imperative that you are constantly aware of your energy around animals.

Unblock the Anxiety Holes

Probably the most vivid description we can use to picture this issue, although perhaps a little stomach-churning, is that of a blocked drain. When a drain is blocked and you continue to flush things down it, it gets backed up. A solid blockage is not going anywhere without some persistent assistance, and if we continue using the drain without cleaning out the blockage, nothing moves, everything backs up and we are eventually left with a very disgusting mess.

Anxiety is considered one of the four blockages to happiness. The other three are guilt, depression and anger. Anxiety can, in some small percentage of cases, be driven by biological factors such as brain chemistry. In the bulk of cases, however, anxiety is driven by thought. As we previously discussed, the anxiety process consists of a trigger, a thought or reaction to the trigger and the behavior that follows. Our anxiety holes are really clogged up with the second part of that equation: the thinking. It is not the trigger nor the behavior that is really the problem but our thoughts about the trigger which results in the behavior.

In order to analyze your thoughts, you need to apply the ELF enquiry method. The ELF enquiry stands for empirical, logical and functional. The empirical assessment of your thought is done by asking yourself if that thought is fact or fiction. You should also be sure that you are differentiating between your reality, which is based on your perceptions and past experiences, and actual reality. The second assessment is whether your thinking is logical. Does your thinking follow a logical line of thought and does your thinking make sense? The final enquiry of your thought is to determine its function. Does it serve a purpose? Does the purpose of the thought serve you in the best way possible (How to Control Anxiety, 2015)?

The nature of anxiety is a constant rumination of past regrets and guilt. It is also the rumination of future fears, which have not yet come to pass and, indeed, may never come to pass. Anxious thoughts will create an energy within you that is unhealthy. This anxious energy, if left untreated and unaddressed, can cause blockages in our psyche and emotional state. The universe is in a constant state of flow and as we are part of the universe, we need to be able to flow with it. If we consider that mindfulness, our panacea to anxiety, is about letting thoughts and feelings flow in without judgement and flow out without refrain, it stands to reason that unresolved anxiety blockages will halt that flow. If you are particularly struggling to attain a state of mindfulness, it may be wise to first start with cleansing these blockages.

Visualize

Visualize a hole that is blocked up with negative gunge. How you picture the gunge is up to you. It could just be a dark matter, or you may find it more useful to picture the blockage as the person, event or thought that you are aware is causing the blockage. Then visualize a bright white bolt of light piercing through the blockage and rushing through you. The white light pushes all the negative gunge away from you and your hole or portal is free to experience energy flow once again (Baron, 2015).

Breathing Exercises

This will also involve a form of visualization. Using one of the mindful breathing techniques we discussed earlier, you can imagine your inhalation breaths as powerful tornadoes that are entering your body and blowing clean all of the blockages you are experiencing. Then, your exhalation breath will be an equally powerful wind that pushes all of the gunge out of your body and away from your energy fields.

Chip Away at It

Your anxiety blockage didn't develop overnight and it certainly won't be cleared in one fell swoop either. We can, however, make small, persistent dents in the blockage on a daily basis until it is completely clear. But while doing so we must ensure that we do not add to the blockage at all. Small efforts of energy cleansing, meditation, mindfulness, consistent gratitude and self-awareness will chip away at the blockage until it is clear. If you feel lighter than you did yesterday, you're doing an excellent job.

Finally at Peace

Inner peace can seem like a far-off magical destination when we are in the clutches of anxiety. It is, however, absolutely possible to reach such a place within ourselves. But what we must remember is that it will only be a permanent state if we work at it. Just as the universe is constantly in a state of flow, so is our inner peace. The harder we work at learning how to easily reattain that state, though, the more time we can spend at peace.

Children, in general, are instinctively at peace. Very small children have no understanding of the concept of yesterday or tomorrow, they all naturally live in the here and now. It is only as we start to near our teenage years that the thoughts of the world around us start to intrude on our minds. It is also at this time in our lives that we are starting to understand that there is a very strict set of societal rules that we are expected to follow. It is suddenly frowned upon to run naked across the lawn or have chocolate icing all over your face.

Ironically, although we know that living in the moment is the key to happiness, the entire world is geared toward keeping us constantly focused on the future. We spend twelve years in school with the promise that when we finish, we will be able to go to university or college. We spend another three or four years in a university or college with the promise that when we finish, we will get a good job. When we get the job, we start saving for the promise of a car, a house and a family. When we have those things, we spend our weeks looking forward to the weekend so that we can spend two days enjoying the things we worked so hard to earn. Then we are promised that if we continue to work until age 65, we will be able to retire. Is there any wonder that we, as a society, find it difficult to live in the moment when the entire world seems to be constantly working toward something just out of reach?

It seems a rather depressing prospect, doesn't it? Well, maybe it is the test. It is so easy to become wrapped up in the rat race and run the hamster wheel that perhaps the real challenge now is to buck the societal norms and build our own version of happiness. Perhaps inner peace is on the other side of us deciding that we don't need the stuff that society tells us we need. Inner peace may just be on the other side of the question: What do I really want?

Inner peace will be a different state for everyone, and you are the only one that will be able to say for sure whether you have attained this state. There are general ways to acknowledge inner peace and while these will not always be the same for everyone, many who feel that they achieved inner peace report the following as the signposts they saw on their inner peace journey:

- **Your responses are more spontaneous:** Your responses to triggers or events, while measured and intentional, are also no longer based on past fears or anxiety about the future. You are able to respond in healthy ways and your responses are proportionate to the event.

- **You are easily able to enjoy the moment:** Your experiences are no longer colored or distracted by events, fears or anxieties about what has been or what may be. You are able to fully immerse yourself in the here and now. You won't spend your Sunday night worrying about work on Monday morning or your Thursday longing for the release of Friday.

- **You have a deeper experience of love:** You find it easier to accept love and care from others and you are able to show love and affection more easily. For many people who have been damaged in their childhood, their experience of love is skewed. They may not believe that they deserve love, or they may feel that they are incapable of properly showing it.

• **You no longer seek to judge others:** You have reached a place where you no longer see any value in judging others for their actions. You are able to accept that others are on their own path and their actions are not a reflection on you, nor can you control what they do or who they are. You can only control your response.

• **You smile more:** One of the greatest myths is that we need a reason to smile. When you achieve a state of inner peace, it becomes easier to simply smile at the beauty of everything you witness. Smiling is no longer a response or reaction but rather a sense of being.

• **Feelings of connectedness:** You will feel more connected to other living beings and nature. It will be easier for you to understand how you fit into the bigger picture and the role that you and others play in the universe (Ortner, 2015). You will also find it easier to connect with complete strangers without the fear that accompanies societal norms.

Chapter 15: How Mindfulness Can Help?

Mindfulness is a way to mental health and well-being which entails utilizing the senses to listen to what is happening around you and inside you at here and now. Unlike anxiety that is centered on coming possibilities and hypotheticals mindfulness is actually around the present moment. Mindfulness instructs you to live in the earth, while nervousness causes you to live trapped in your mind, centered on your spinning ideas and feelings. With mindfulness then you may:

•Keep your mind occupied with what's real, leaving less room for anxious, racing thoughts and negative customs.

•Replace stress with joy and durabllity.

•Take back what anxiety gets stolen from you such as enjoying friendships or romantic relationships without worrying about doing something wrong. You'll be able to visit your kids' activities without being on border and complete a school or work assignment without fearing that it is not good enough.

In our daily lives, we often face sophistication, problems, pressure and other types of anxiety. We're so busy and in a hurry doing things, anticipate another problem or another fantastic situation to occur that we forget that the beauty of the current moment which is unfolding in front of our eyes.

Mindfulness will help us slow down, even live our own life incomplete and thus feel happier. In addition, it can help improve our disposition and the way we live.

You may have heard of mindfulness earlier and not understand what it is about or perhaps you never heard of it but anyway do not worry in either case at the conclusion of this guide, I expect you'll have a fantastic idea of exactly what mindfulness is even the mindfulness benefits and a few simple techniques to start practicing mindfulness immediately.

You'll have a decision to begin practicing it or not.

I keep reminding others that it is very important not to quit learning but we must put to practice what we learn because if we don't take any action, nothing will change in our life.

Advantages of mindfulness

Dwelling in a mindful way will help:

Have a stronger concentration and focus.

Reduce tension, nervousness and stress.

Clear thinking and not as emotional turmoil.

Lower blood pressure and cholesterol.

Support in kicking along with other self-defeating behaviors.

Greater creativity and enhanced functionality in play and work.

Increased self-understanding, self-acceptance and self-esteem.

More joy, love and spontaneity.

Greater intimacy with family and friends members.

A deeper awareness of significance and purpose. (How to locate purpose in life?)

Glimpses of a spiritual dimension of being.

Giving more attention to the present moment to your thoughts and feelings but also to the whole world around you can improve your mental well-being. You may consider health in terms of everything you have: your earnings, home or car or your project but the evidence shows that what we do and how we believe has the greatest impact on well-being. Good mental well-being means feeling good about yourself and about life and being able to move on with life as you wish.

How mindfulness techniques help with anxiety?

For our purposes, the most essential point to keep in mind about mindfulness is the fact that it functions. Be assured in the truth that the study supports the efficacy of mindfulness for reducing stress. For an example, the University of California, Los Angeles researchers examined a number of studies and found that mindfulness benefits the mind by protecting us from stress and enhancing our decision-making methods. In a 2011 study reported from psychiatry Research: Neuro-imaging researchers found that practicing mindfulness affects the brain in positive ways like increasing gray matter (regions of the brain containing nerve cell bodies). Among the many areas comprised of grey matter is that the hippocampus, a structure involved in learning, memory, psychological control and anxiety stimulation and responsiveness. The hippocampus is one of those parts of the brain responsible for anxiety. Through mindfulness, the study's researchers report we could raise the grey matter in the hippocampus, effectively strengthening it and allow it to better withstand stress and thus reduce anxiety.

So, we have established that mindfulness certainly works to decrease anxiety and that means it is possible to reclaim your life and live fully and freely. But its plans can be difficult to learn and they're able to take some getting used to. Anxiety is used to having a good deal of control over your mind and it won't give up its energy easily. You may experience frustration and uncertainty along the way. Can I do this right? Why do I still feel anxious? Why is it that no matter what I would do, my mind will not stay focused and goes right back into ruminating and fretting? These are typical questions and challenges people face when learning to decrease anxiety through mindfulness practices. Know these ideas and many others like them are normal and par for the program. Learning how to employ mindfulness is a procedure over a quick cure though which you will probably feel some subtle adjustments right away. Nevertheless, there are means to shift your thinking regarding this process that will make your mindfulness journey more enjoyable and less irritating.

Let these mental skills lightly guide you as you progress through this workbook.

Nonjudgment: Anxious ideas involve rules, absolutes instead of berating to perceived flaws, strategy the present instant without cluttering it.

Patience: Be kind to yourself as you build a mindful way of life understanding that it is a process with plenty of stops and starts.

Beginner's Head: Approach your anxious thoughts with all the mind-set of a beginner, someone who does not have all of the answers? That way when anxiety attempts to convince you of something, you're offered to the simple fact there are different chances.

Additional Researchers have discovered that "Mindfulness Meditation Programs" specifically can reduce the negative dimensions of emotional anxiety, including stress in a broad assortment of clinical problems. They concluded that within 2 weeks to eight months, the consequences were clinically modest but "like what one might expect from the use of an antidepressant at a primary care population".

In 2011, Harvard researchers found that just eight months of MBSR by participants decreased the volume of brain tissues in the amygdala which is the portion of the brain responsible for stress, anxiety, fear and stress. The participants were psychologically healthy adults searching for anxiety reduction, who hadn't taken over 10 meditation courses in their own lives and not one in the previous six weeks. According to the researchers, the results indicate that MBSR aids the brain to elaborate in areas related to person self-referentiality, viewpoints and regulation of emotion.

It seems that MBSR can lower our propensity to react automatically and compulsively to events in our own lives. MBSR therefore can be helpful for people suffering not just from generalized anxiety disorder but also from social anxiety disorder (SAD). Individuals with SAD tend to have problems with psychological regulation and frequently experience twisted views of these. An analysis comparing the benefits of MBSR with aerobic exercise in people with SAD discovered that meditation has been associated with a decline in the severity of signs and a higher ability to control adverse auto talk.

Studies have also proven that meditation rewires the links between the medial prefrontal cortex, the part of the brain which processes information about oneself and the areas of the brain that control sensation and fear. Someone who practices meditation is often better able to dismiss any sensations that might otherwise have caused anxiety. The neural pathways that connect to all those upsetting sensations are diminished.

Another analysis conducted at Yale Faculty provides an insight to the potential neural elements of meditation. Researchers discovered that meditation reduces activity in the Default Mode Network

(DMN), also called the "monkey mind", thus called since it's more energetic when our heads quickly change from thought to thought. From the analysis, the principal nodes of the DMN were discovered comparatively deactivated in seasoned meditators. Moreover, brain regions related to self-control and cognitive management were related in people practicing meditation.

Meditation and other awareness-based therapies have attracted the attention of the public and researchers because they provide an antidote comparatively free of side effects to the feverish challenges of our daily lives. There are a few reservations yet: a study into the possible negative consequences of meditation and consciousness remains insufficient, for example; some researchers say, the potential for worsening symptoms of stress and other mental disorders in certain people but the tradition of consciousness cannot be considered a cure for the numerous types of anxiety that many of us experience, research shows for many people calming the brain even if just for a few minutes a day may cause a decrease in stress and stress, to greater self-control and to a diminished inclination to take things personally. We may not be in a position to control what happens in the outside world but we know that we've got some control over how we respond to it and that the tools to do so are within ourselves.

Utilizing mindfulness for anxiety will become a way of life. This book will guide you along your path to peace of mind.

Mindfully deal with complex emotions

Let's get real here. For nearly all of us, including myself, existence is fast-paced and chock filled with family, relationship and work stressors. In fact, along with the ever-increasing pressures of society and technology at large, it can really have a toll on your union.

Consequently, hard feelings like anger, confusion, anxiety, isolation and sadness just to mention a few can arise. Emotions such as these are usually the very current and effective forces in your life.

The key to beat these hard feelings is mindfulness! Practicing mindfulness allows you to relax and soothe your self. In this state, you've got room to reflect and thoughtfully respond instead of reacting.

Following six steps will help you to comprehend and cope with your hard feelings in a manner that is aware:

Measure 1: Turn toward your own emotions with acceptance.

After you become aware of the emotion you are feeling, detect where it is in your body. You might feel it as a stomachache, a tightening of your neck, the pounding of the heart or even stress someplace. Sit with this anger, anxiety, depression, despair, guilt, sadness, shame or whatever emotion you're having. Become conscious of it and do not discount it. If this is tough, wake up and walk around or get a cup of tea.

The key is to not push the emotion away. Bottling it up inside is only going to result in it to bubble up as well as explode later causing much more difficult emotions or perhaps a full mental shut-down. Listen to your hard emotions. They are trying to help you awaken to what is going on prior to a major catastrophe occurs.

Step 2: Recognize and label the emotion.

Instead of saying,"I am angry", say: "That really is anger" or "this is stress". In this way, you're acknowledging its existence while simultaneously enabling you to remain isolated from it.

When my husband was at the hospital until he passed, I felt a profound sense of uncertainty, stress and dread. I needed to acknowledge and recognize the emotions and say to myself, "I know that I am experiencing anxiety and fear right now and I really don't know what's going to happen but I am likely to just be with it". Though it remained a very painful experience towards the conclusion, identifying and tagging my emotions in this way allowed me to take some of this hassle from what I was feeling. Then this let me stay in the present compared to catapulting me into the future or trapping me before. Being thrust in either direction could have just induced me to blame myself. I can only imagine how that important voice could have spelled out, "If you would have done anything differently perhaps there could have been a different outcome."

Step 3: Accept your emotions.

When you're feeling a particular emotion, do not deny it. Acknowledge and admit the emotion actually exists, while it's nervousness, grief, sadness or perhaps whatever you are having in that second. Through mindful acceptance, it is possible to adopt difficult feelings of compassion, consciousness and understanding involving your own partner.

Think of a friend or a loved one who might be having a hard time. What could you say to them? Bring the situation of what you would say to them into your mind. Now, say exactly the identical thing to yourself: "I'm ok. I'm not to blame. I really did the best I can." Hold these images and phrases within your self with loving kindness and empathy. Extend this particular act of kindness toward yourself and be conscious of what is happening in you. In this manner, you will gain the ability to not just calm and soothe yourself but also your partner.

You will soon come to understand that you are not your rage, fear, despair or any other difficult emotion you are feeling. Rather you will start to experience these feelings in a timelier manner such as clouds that pass by in the heavens. Opening yourself up for your emotions permits you to make a space of awareness, curiosity and expansiveness that you could subsequently apply to your connection in addition to any other aspect of your own life.

Step 4: Realize the impermanence of your emotions.

Every one of your emotions is impermanent. They appear and reside within you for a time, then disappear. It's easy to overlook that if you are in the middle of dealing with difficult emotions.

Allow yourself to witness and watch your emotions with kind patience and attention, giving them the latitude to unfold and in many cases, completely vanish. To adopt this procedure ask yourself:

"Where and what is this sense?"

"What do I need now?"

"How do I nurture it?"

"What do I do for my partner?"

"What can my partner do?"

"How do we, as a few, flip toward one another using acts of loving-kindness?"

Asking these focused questions and responding subsequently will go quite a ways to promote compassion, compassion and link within your connection.

Step 5: Inquire and investigate.

After you have calmed and soothed yourself by the impact of your feelings have a little time to delve deep and explore what occurred. Ask yourself the following questions:

"What triggered me personally?"

"What's causing me to feel like this?"

"What is the discomfort I'm experiencing and where can it be originating?"

"Was it the result of my critical mind or was it in reaction to something my partner did or said?"

Perhaps you had a tough day on the job or difficulty dealing with your loved ones. Perhaps you feel dizzy, lonely or disconnected because of your interactions with somebody. Whatever the cause or trigger, look at it closely and ask yourself what is occurring here. Think about what was said or done and compare it for your own values:

What have you been to, your expectations surrounding the circumstances?

What reactions or judgments caused one to become angry or anxious?

Can it be a pattern that keeps appearing?

Asking these essential questions and investigating the root of your difficult emotions will help you acquire empathy and insight to what you are having.

Taking yourself off and trusting that your deepest, authentic self to answer these questions about your situation will make a room to see things with another perspective. This will ultimately allow both you and your spouse to be present and connected with one another.

Step 6: Let go of the need to control your feelings

The key to mindful coping with your hard emotions would be to let go of your need to restrain them. Instead be amenable to the result and what functions. Step outside yourself and really hear what your spouse is feeling and what he or she must say. Only then will you truly gain an in-depth understanding of your feelings and also the connections surrounding them within your connection.

Mindfully dealing with feelings is difficult and it takes time. Make kind, compassionate and patient with your own spouse. You're in this together.

We're lucky that we live in a world where you and your spouse can choose the time to explore, discuss, and learn about mindfulness and your own emotions. Require nothing for granted because life is fragile and fleeting!

Chapter 16: Have A Mind Of Your Own

When the teachings of life lessons and personal growth are so simplistic, sometimes you take a look at it, and the very next moment, you move on repeating the same negative habits. Many habits (especially new ones) require repetition, focus and concentration, to condition the brain to di-gest and remember, to rewire, reset and reboot the system. It takes consistent personal effort and that moment of lining up with that decision to eliminate things, tasks, people, that consumes and drains you to no end. Or else, there isn't really many changes to your current pat-tern of thoughts and the way you carry yourself in your day-to-day.

You're always tired, emotionally drained, and a chore to be with, always dumping your problems and issues onto other people. Or vice-versa, having people do that to you. What goes around, comes around. That's what a vicious cycle is. You get back the exact same thing you put out there for others. That — is the balance of nature. It circles right back to you. You are still giving away what you don't have, I call it having your emotions "in deficit".

Whether you harbor a great insecurity and fear for aging, for your weight, your finances, your relationships, any single one of that (individually) is considered being emotionally tied down, as trivial as it may seem. As long as you carry stress and negative habit of thoughts about any single aspect of your life, you are not completely "free". If it pops up in your head constantly and lingers around, you are not free.

Most people just grow accustomed to all these negative feelings over a period that it eventually feels "normal" to have it stick around in their life experience. When was the last time you said or heard, "someone said the other day... someone told me last week... I heard from someone..." over your conversations? If that "someone" isn't you, keep it to yourself and don't pass it on to anyone. Even if that someone is your mother. Especially if it is your mother. If you've never tasted it, tried it, felt it yourself, don't tell someone what "someone else" said. That's like trying to feed a person food that your own pet dog wouldn't even steal a sniff. If you haven't even tasted it, don't offer it to someone else.

Don't blindly believe everything you see and hear without experiencing it for yourself to see that it truly serves you well too, and don't doubt anything you've never seen or heard before, at the first chance without trying and simply write it off without thinking twice. In short, have a mind of your own. A strong and sturdy one that will tide you through the harshest of conditions. Making the shift (learning how to) to make the decision to follow your own heart (and own mind) lays the foundation to customize yourself a belief system that serves you well. Permanently.

Self-love and worthiness is validated not by the compliments people pay you, but from your own acceptance to love and honor yourself completely. Each time you feel the need to hear a praise feel good about yourself, you shoot yourself in the foot and when you constantly need someone's approval to appreciate your very own self, you will never ever feel free for the rest of your life.

Chapter 17: The Three Poisons

In life, there are three poisons that can lead you towards carrying an enormous amount of emotional baggage. These poisons are ones that are easy to become entangled in, especially if you are not mindful of your thoughts. They are persistent, and once you allow yourself to fall into the pattern of one, the other two will inevitably surface. You will be lead down a path of continuously growing emotional baggage until you become aware of this cycle and develop mindfulness around it. Only then will you be able to relieve yourself from these three poisons and return to a pure mind and heart.

The Three Poisons are the cause of all human suffering, according to Buddhism. They include greed, anger, and ignorance. Whenever you read or hear about these traits, they are called the fundamental evils or the Three Poisons. These are dangerous toxins that exist in life and we must learn to eliminate them if we desire to carry on down the path to Nirvana. Under each of the Three Poisons are additional branches of said poison that can further damage your purity and carry you deeper into the toxicity of their existence.

Anger

The first of the Three Poisons is anger. This poison is accompanied by hatred, aversion, and animosity. When you are affected by greed, you may notice you are experiencing symptoms of the previous three emotions, as well as hostility, dislike, or ill-will when you are wishing harm of any sort upon another person. When you are experiencing this poison, you may find that you are resisting against many things. You will be in denial and likely will avoid any feelings that are unpleasant to you. The things you avoid may include people, places, things or specific situations. When you are being affected by this poison, you wish for everything to be satisfying all of the time. You crave and desire only comfort and pleasantness. When you are infected with this toxin, you will find that you only seem to discover more anger and hatred in your life. You are likely never calm, as you are always feeling as though you need to protect yourself from others. You fail to be able to clearly understand life for what it is and carry negative and pessimistic judgments against everything that occurs. You will likely also be creating a significant amount of your own discomfort and conflict within' yourself as a result of having an aversion to all that makes you feel uncomfortable and therefore resisting things that are important to your growth and wellbeing. When you are infected with the poison of hatred, you will find that you are consistently creating conflict and that you seem to have a number of enemies around you and within' you.

Greed

The second of the Three Poisons is greed. When you are greedy, you have what they call an "unquenchable third" (tahna) or intense craving for the objects you desire. You feel as though the objects you desire or the situation you desire will bring you long and lasting fulfillment, that it will make you feel whole or somehow complete. As a result, you develop a hunger for possessions or situations that ends with you striving for a goal that you will never attain because you will always set the bar higher and higher. When you are intoxicated with the poison of greed, you believe that your happiness is dependent upon you reaching a goal, and you will constantly look outside of you for things that can only be developed within' you. Greed is the never ending chase for instant gratifications that provide you with fleeting insights of the feelings you crave: happiness, joy, fulfillment, and peace. Eventually, though, greed leads to emptiness. Even the situations that once gave you fleeting happiness will eventually cease to bring you anything, and you will continually chase a feeling that is no longer available to be acquired from outside of you. You will be forced to turn inward to discover them again, should you decide to lead a life with these fundamental things we all truly want.

When you experience symptoms of greed, you will be compulsive, destructive, and impulsive. You will constantly want more and you will make instantaneous decisions with the intention to bring yourself more. You will not be thinking for your highest good, nor will you be thinking for the collective good of humankind. When you are affected by greed, it affects you on a number of different levels. It affects your success, your personal life, and your inner life. We can see the effects of greed on the globe through warfare and global conflict, which are obvious symptoms of the corporate and political greed within' our Earth. It is important that we do not fall into the path of greed, and that if we do we become mindful of our situation and break it immediately. Doing this will eliminate this poison from you and take away the suffering that is attached with greed. You will then be able to work towards a purer mind, heart, body and soul.

Ignorance

The final and possibly worst of the Three Poisons is ignorance or delusion. When we fall into a pattern of ignorance, we fall into one of the most toxic of all of the poisons. Ignorance leads to further anger and greed, which can lead to further ignorance, and take you deep into a spiral of unwanted toxicity and poison. When you are in a state of ignorance, you will be carrying a misperception of reality and the way the world works. You will fail to understand the way things actually are, and you will be influenced by your ignorance. In this state, you lack harmony with yourself, others, and the world around you. You are not able to understand the way life is interdependent and lacks permanence, therefore you will constantly look outside of yourself for happiness (greed). As you find that you are not able to discover that which you desire most, you will become frustrated and full of hatred (anger). Ignorance is the final state where you slide on the downward spiral of increasing greed and anger, and thus increasing ignorance.

When you reach the state of ignorance, you selfmanifest infinitely more greed and anger into your life on an even faster level than you would if you were void of ignorance. As a result, you will find that you are constantly attracting more and more negativity to yourself, and you will not have an easy time eliminating this emotional baggage from your mind. You will be deeply affected by the Three Poisons, and it will take a large situation to eliminate these from your life. Until you can become awakened to your ignorance, you will never be able to free yourself from the Three Poisons.

The root to all emotional baggage in life is the Three Poisons. When you are infected by either of the three or any combination, you will be left with a large amount of emotional baggage that weighs heavy in your life. You will struggle to find peace and purity in your life and as a result, you will feel heavy and ill at all times. You will fail to be at harmony with yourself and the life that surrounds you, and you will have no hope of achieving nirvana.

If you recognize any of these Three Poisons in your life, it is important that you start becoming mindful around them and that you start eliminating them from your life. Eliminating them does not mean that you will not feel anger, greed, or ignorance in your life. It means that you will become aware of the situations that trigger those feelings and you will be able to act intentionally and purposefully to prevent yourself from feeding into either of them and increasing their negative impact on your life. Instead of being owned by your feelings, you will own your feelings and you will be able to powerfully control them and thus eliminate any major impact that they may have on you should you fail to recognize them.

Chapter Summary:

- There are Three Poisons in life
- The Three Poisons are anger, greed, and ignorance
- You can be infected by one, two, or all three of these poisons
- They prevent you from achieving purity or nirvana
- Ignorance is the worst, as it magnifies anger and greed

Chapter 18: Mindfulness Technique #3:

Curating Your Thoughts

As I've mentioned in the previous chapter, the runaway horse effect has a stage where your mind chooses to pick up on certain details and overlook others. This is a tremendously important step in the runaway horse effect because what you choose to dwell on impacts the information that you will interpret. These interpretations, in turn, trigger certain emotions.

Once, you get past the emotion stage, it's really almost impossible to change course because these emotions trigger actions as well. You end up saying things that you might regret later on. You might start making decisions that may not be all that good for you in the long run. All sorts of less than optimal things can happen because you are simply clueless regarding this chain of events.

Thought curation is all about taking control of the first part of this chain

As mentioned in the discussion regarding the runaway horse effect in the previous chapter, once you reach the stage of emotional triggers, it's almost impossible to take control over the runaway horse. It takes a tremendous amount of self-control, self-knowledge, and awareness to make a dent in the almost foregone conclusion of how you would react once you get past the emotional stage.

You can achieve a tremendous amount of control over your emotional triggers by looking at the first stage of this chain of events. If you apply thought curation to the first stage, then you can pretty much dictate what you will choose to interpret, which then affects your emotional state, which then in turn dictates how you will act.

It's all about cherry-picking your reality

Most people look at the first stage of the runaway horse effect as something that is a foregone conclusion. They assume at the back of their heads that it's just something that happens. They don't understand the fact that this is actually a habit. Just because you have a habit of smoking doesn't necessarily mean that you're doomed to constantly smoke. The same goes with alcoholism or drug addiction.

Every day there are people who break the chain of smoking. You could be one of those people if you choose to. It's a choice, and unfortunately, too many people think that the first stage that involves picking up on certain signals is completely natural or is set in stone. That is absolute garbage. That's nonsense and there's no truth to that.

You see, your mind is like sponge. As you grow up, you start picking up on different habits. If you were not careful, you might have picked up certain habits along the way (maybe from your parents) that don't really help you.

What you choose to dwell on is an effect of habit. I need you to realize this. I need you to wrap your mind around this, otherwise, you won't be able to make mindfulness technique numbers 2 and 3 work for you. It's just not going to happen.

You have to understand that you can break that habit. Just because you've been doing things the same way for a long, long time doesn't necessarily mean that you would have to continue doing things the same way. You can choose to make a break today. You can choose to be more deliberate in how you choose to dwell on the different data points your mind picks up at any given point in time.

You're always judging your thoughts

Once you've cherry-picked your data points, the next stage as I've mentioned previously is that you judge them. Again, people do this habitually. They think that there's only one conclusion once a certain data point comes in.

If you see a house burning in front of you, if you're like most people, in your mind there's only one conclusion. The possibility of a planned burning or a test burning escapes most people. They automatically assume that this house is burning out because there was an accidental fire and it's the end of the world. People freak out.

Always remember that you're judging your thoughts and that these data points have been chosen by your mind. They did not just materialize out of nowhere. You actually have a direct hand whether you choose to recognize it or not, or whether you choose to be conscious of it or not, when picking those points of information.

Be aware of these two processes. Be aware that you're always cherry-picking your reality. Be mindful of the fact that you're always judging your thoughts. If you are able to do this, then you have set in motion the process with which you can break free of the chains of emotional reaction.

If you feel that you're stuck in your life or you keep making the wrong decisions, as far as money, relationships, health are concerned, it's because of this chain reaction. The good news is by curating your thoughts, you can make a break. You can break that chain.

Maybe you're not as good with emotional control as with other parts of the runaway horse chain, it's okay. As long as you break the chain at some point, you will make progress.

How thought curation works

Thought curation is all about breaking the chain that I mentioned above. You do this by simply grabbing hold of a single thought. That's it. You just take a thought and then you strip it apart. You demonstrate to yourself, in no uncertain terms, that certain images don't have to have power over you.

Like most people, when you see certain mental images you start assuming that it has to mean something and this leads to an emotional reaction. This is like a slip second assumption. Most people aren't even aware of this. This just happens. Well, when you apply mindfulness technique number 3, you grab hold of a single thought and you focus all your analytical firepower on it. You start stripping it apart.

You start asking yourself, "What are the possible ways I can interpret this? Why did I pick this up instead of another thought? Why did this come to be?" By simply hitting it from many different angles with all these questions, you achieve two things. First, you slow down the runaway horse effect. You're not just jumping from image to value judgment, or to emotional reaction, or to physical action.

The second thing that you do is that you destroy the helplessness that you often feel when judging mental images. You shed a bright light of logic and reason to how you normally "automatically" think. This can be a very empowering exercise because you are left with emotion-free thoughts.

You can see mental images without the emotional baggage. You would be able to analyze them from many different perspectives and not feel that you are emotionally bound to come to some sort of conclusion.

By being free from emotional requirements of these mental images, you can then start making better decisions. At the very least, you would be calm. You would feel less stressed. You would feel that things can be solved and that things are possible again.

The best result that emotion-free thoughts bring to the table however is that you would be able to look at the things that you choose to pick up and create new connections with them. Maybe a certain perception that you get, for example, when your loved one says a certain phrase and you automatically feel that he or she no longer loves you, and this triggers an emotional downward spiral.

When you use this mindfulness technique and you curate that thought and strip it of its previously negative interpretation, you can then switch a new interpretation to it or plug it in to other thoughts.

Instead of feeling crappy or fearful that a breakup is imminent when your boyfriend or girlfriend, or husband or wife, says a certain sentence, you can choose to be more analytical about it. You can use a more logical interpretation. Maybe the reason they're saying that is because they too are hurting. Maybe they too feel that there's something missing in your relationship.

This is a tremendous opportunity for you to engage in genuine conversations instead of looking at their statements solely from your perspective. Instead of being so completely self-absorbed, you start moving towards a center point where you can engage in a genuine conversation and this may take your relationship to the next level.

This analysis can also apply to other things going on in your life. Maybe your boss sometimes sends certain signals that throw you off and make you panic. Perhaps adopting this mindfulness technique enables you to look at the situation in a more neutral manner so you can come up with a response that would lead to more positive results for your career.

This applies all across the board and the great thing about curating your thoughts is that it takes control of the runaway horse while it's still in the barn. You're not left in a situation where the horse has already ran out of the barn and is already bolting or is already in the field and you're just going to burn yourself out running after it and jumping on its back.

Of course, this technique won't be easy at first. In many cases, people have mental processes that are like fire hydrants. There is just so much volume coming out. But with enough practice, you would be able to slow down the fire hydrant and take more control over the data that's coming out and eventually come up with a system that works very smoothly and that makes you feel you have a tremendous amount of personal control.

Chapter 19: Belief System Exercise

Each of us has a unique set of belief systems. The people that you work with for example may have different religions. Sometimes, our firm belief in each system makes us judgmental and close-minded. A mind in the mindful state is neither of the two.

In this exercise, we will practice putting ourselves in other people's shoes. In one of your rest periods, you should take the time to step away from the crowd and meditate. When meditating, you should breathe deeply and make your mind become calm.

When your mind is calm, you should look for a person that you often interact with. Identify a belief system where you and that person disagree. For example, he could be a republican while you are a democrat or vice versa. He could also be Christian while you are a Jew.

After identifying your target, you should try to imagine yourself in that person's shoes and believing his or her belief system. First, you should imagine what that person believes in.

Next, you should imagine how different things are because you change your belief system. It is important that you do this exercise without judging the other person or his or her belief system.

Lastly, you should observe your target's behavior. You should identify the traits that he has that directly come from the belief system that you focused on.

People who do this exercise often become surprised of what they discover just by considering other people's belief systems. Most people would not even try this exercise because they do not want to be converted.

In times, certain parts of other people's belief systems will make us emotional. We may exhibit signs of annoyance or hate. We may even begin to resent our target because of their belief system. When you encounter this experience, you should stop the exercise and do your breath counting exercise to lessen the degree of your emotions and calm down. However, in our case, we are not trying to convince ourselves that our belief system is better or worse than other people. We are merely examining how these beliefs affect the people around us.

In most cases, doing this activity makes you more mindful of the behavior of other people around you.

Instead of thinking thoughts like 'why cannot you be more like me', people who try this exercise end up trying to understand the people around them.

Chapter 20: The Bad And Ugly

Stress, anxiety and worry all originate in our minds. It is our thoughts that create the hell. Mindfulness will help you in this aspect, and it is very exciting to know that something so simple can have such a profound impact on our lives! But sometimes when we are ready to start something new and healthy in our lives, we are gung ho at first; and then we easily can slip back to our old ways of doing things. We can't let that happen this time. Mindfulness is so easy and so beneficial; there is no way to continue living without it in your daily life.

First let's get this bad stuff out of the way. You need to see this because you really have to see where all of this useless stress, worry and anxiety can land you if you don't get it under control. When you see the big picture that could unfold, it will give you the motivation to find time each day to continue your Mindfulness.

Having uncontrolled stress and anxiety in your life can cause:

Aging (faster than normal)

Alzheimer's Disease

Asthma

Depression

Diabetes

Dizziness

Fatigue

Gastrointestinal Problems (like GERD, IBS, etc.)

Headaches

Heart Disease

Irritability

Muscle Aches and Tension

Nausea

Obesity

Premature Death

Prone to Drug and/or Alcohol Abuse

Rapid Breathing or Shortness of Breath

Relationship Issues

Sleep Problems

Suppression of Immune System

Trembling and Twitching

And more…

Now take a deep breath. Feel that breath enter your body, and now exhale. This is a list of very severe ailments; but do not stress or worry about it anymore. You are about to embark on a journey that can not only prevent these things from happening, but enhance your life in ways you can't even imagine right now.

Now let's get to the good stuff. There is hope, and it is in Mindfulness.

When asked how Mindfulness has alleviated stress, worry or anxiety for our experts, this is what they had to say:

"It gives me a different perspective in which to interpret a given situation rather than the most common one, which is reactivity." Franne D.

"This is where the practice has been really helpful to me. In the past, my mind would always go to the worst-case scenario. Once I learned the true meaning of the saying "where awareness goes, energy flows," I became more aware of my thoughts, and how my thoughts trigger my feelings. I learned that when I keep my awareness on my discomfort, or the thoughts that triggered my discomfort, that feeling grows. And when I take my awareness off of the stress, worry, or anxiety that I am feeling, it immediately begins to alleviate any discomfort I am experiencing. Even though every situation is different, I can say that most of the time, simply choosing a different focus or perspective transforms my experience. As I become calmer, I can begin to reflect on the thoughts that triggered me and I can determine whether or not they are true for me or the situation I find myself in at the moment. Most of the time they are not. With that realization, I can choose to be accepting of what is, and when possible, I choose new thoughts or perspectives that are more in alignment with me and / or the situation I am experiencing." Dana C.

Along the same fragrant note, by alleviating stress, worry, and/or anxiety, peace will be a beautiful byproduct. This is what our experts said when asked how Mindfulness helped them find that peace in their lives:

"By softening my heart and changing how I view everything." Franne D.

"Choosing to slow down and just be was initially challenging. I had no idea how busy my mind was, and how judgmental and negative my thoughts could be. At first, that awareness made me more anxious. But as I continued to practice, the anxiety fell away as I chose to place my awareness on other things: my breath, the pose, the inspirational quotes my teacher read, the music she played. Over time, my mind became quieter as I practiced focusing my awareness on the present moment. The practice now gives me the space and time I need to neutrally observe what is going on around and within me. When I shift my awareness into an observer mode, I notice the thoughts and beliefs, judgments and perceptions that keep me from experiencing peace. In that moment, I can reflect on whether or not these thoughts are true for me, and I can also choose to look at my situation from a different point of view. Giving myself this time and space to reflect on my experience shifts my thoughts and feelings in positive ways. Taking responsibility for my reactions is empowering. I know that I can choose to keep the thoughts I like and release or reframe the ones I don't. I constantly remind myself that peace is always available to me. I can continue to suffer, or I can choose peace. It really is that simple." Dana C.

Chapter 21: Mindfulness All Day And Every Day

I just want to be happy. We've uttered this sentence more times than we can count. We continue to pursue it, to yearn for it, to make decisions and act based on what we think may improve our chances at happiness. Happiness, however, will continue to remain an elusive concept until you learn to accept that true happiness can only be attained by initiating change from within. In this case, through mindfulness. Family, career, friends, love, romance, material possessions. As happy as they make you feel in the moment, that happiness will eventually fade away in their absence.

If you continue to pin your happiness on impermanent elements, you will always be disappointed and find yourself back at square one. At the end of the day, lasting happiness, the kind that continues to linger with or without the additional factors, can only be attained when mindfulness is a part of your everyday life. A lot of factors in your life may shift and change as time goes by, but the one thing that can remain a constant is mindful living. All-day and every day.

The Present Is Your Happiest State

It's not your past that makes you the happiest. It's not an unknown future that is going to hold the promise of happiness you long so badly for. Your happiest state is where you are right now. In the present. It is the present where your most meaningful experiences are happening. The past is already behind you, and you can never predict the future with 100% surety. But the present? That's your current reality.

The problem with everyday routine is we've become so used to doing it most of the time we go through the motions without any thought or emotion. We don't stop to appreciate our good health which enables us to carry out these motions in the first place. We don't stop long enough to feel grateful for the familiar surroundings that bring us comfort as we do what we have to do each day. Mindfulness is something you need to carry with you throughout the day, not do it once, twice or several times a day and hope to see a difference. You need to apply mindfulness when you brush your teeth, pick up a glass of water to drink, wait for the train or bus to begin your commute to work, catching up with a friend, texting on the phone. You need to apply mindfulness to everything that you do, that's what it means to make it a part of everyday life.

It seems research agrees that because we spend nearly 50% of the time, we have each day being caught up in our thought process, we're actively contributing to our unhappiness. Instead of being engaged, we drift in and out through the motions aimlessly. Those few moments that we do stop to take stock of? Well, most of the time they're either unpleasant or unhappy, which is how it got our attention in the first place.

Everything that you do is an opportunity for mindfulness and it's time to embrace these moments. Don't worry about emptying your mind of any thoughts or emotions right away, this will gradually happen with practice. What you can do instead to start with is to bring your attention back to focus each time you feel your thoughts drifting.

Mindfulness Begins with Self-Acceptance

Do you accept yourself just as you are right now? Most of the time the answer is going to be no. Most people would even have a long list of things they would either like to change about themselves or their lives. The root cause of a lot of the stress, worry and anxiety that happens stems from feeling like you cannot control the things that are happening around you. You worry because you don't know the outcome and how it is going to affect you. You find it difficult to accept things as they are because you yearn for more.

Being mindful everyday means learning how to accept what comes each day. Accept the things that cause you to stress instead of trying to fight or reject it. Accept that there are some things you cannot control no matter how badly you may want to. Accept that the person you are right now is exactly who you are meant to be. Learn to accept and you will free up a lot of the burden that stress has placed on your shoulders. Acceptance will give you the freedom of not being chained to your stress all the time. You acknowledge that it is there but you will not let it control you. You accept that there will be moments and situations when your worries will flare up again, but you will not let it control you the way it did before.

Begin your mindfulness journey by repeating these phrases to yourself each day:

• **My Stress Does Not Define Me. I Accept My Stress** - Your stressful thoughts do not define who you are as a person. The stressful circumstances you find yourself in do not define your abilities and strengths. What you think and feel right now is only temporary and it is not going to last forever. Accept that this is something you have to go through, be mindful of how it makes you feel. It's easier to deal with anything when you don't attempt to resist as much.

• **I Am Good Enough** - Mindfulness is acceptance. Including accepting who you are completely and wholeheartedly. If you are not going to be okay with being who you are, as you are right now, you are not going to be able to progress very far. You'll struggle with your mindful thoughts every step of the way, feeling like you're never good enough. Accept yourself as you are inside and out and believe it or not, you will feel a sense of relief when you do.

• **I Accept My Strengths and I Accept My Weaknesses** - Being mindful of your strengths and your weaknesses is how you learn to appreciate your strengths even more. Every weakness can be turned into a strength, but not if you stress out about it. It is only through mindful acceptance of both strengths and weaknesses that you can begin developing the mental clarity you need to work on what you believe are your weaknesses.

- **I Am Mindful of Who I Am and I Don't Compare** - Comparison only leads to stress when you pit yourself against those you see as "doing better than you are." You cannot be mindful of your sense of happiness when you're busy comparing yourself to others and thinking about all the things they have that you don't.

Daily Phrases to Remind You to be Mindful

To be mindful is difficult when you feel you're constantly fighting against yourself. Acceptance can be a liberating experience, and you may find that you are more okay with yourself that you thought you were. Through acceptance, you free yourself from the unnecessary strain on negativity.

Set an Intention to Be Mindful Every Day

Establishing intention is one good way of living with a purpose. Instead of stress being your only source of focus throughout the day, isn't it better to have something more productive on your mind to work towards? Why not establish an intention to be mindful instead? Establishing an intention is simple enough in theory. The idea behind this technique is that when you have a goal that you have set actively set for yourself, your focus slowly starts to shift from being worried and anxious all the time and channel that focus towards achieving that goal. For example, if your goal is to be mindful all the way on your commute to work, focus on that instead. The act of establishing a goal – an intention – makes it feel real, and when it does, you're closer to making it come true.

When you wake up in the morning, write a little note to yourself that says my intention today is to spend at least 5-minutes in mindful meditation before heading to work. Look at what you've just written, and acknowledge it. When you've accomplished that goal, notice how much better you feel about yourself, and what a world of difference that can make on your outlook. You accomplished a goal – an intention – that you set out to do.

Establishing an intention is another way of regulating your stress and this is why:

• Setting an intention is not about asking or wishing for something to happen. It's about you taking control of your like and making it happen for yourself.

• When you establish an intention, you're establishing a genuine desire to overcome the challenge you are faced with.

• Your intention is going to serve as your personal reminder about what you want to accomplish.

• Your intention helps with acceptance and acknowledge emotions.

Making Mindfulness a Part of Your Daily Routine

• **Gratitude All Day** - Be grateful. Be so grateful for everything that happens to you throughout the day. Be grateful you woke up this morning healthy. Be grateful you got to work safely. Be grateful you had to means to buy food and drink when you were hungry. Be grateful for another productive day at work. Spend every waking moment being grateful for all the little things in your life, especially the things we tend to overlook. Being grateful is an exercise in mindfulness because it slows you down long enough to stop and appreciate what you were reminding yourself to be grateful for.

- **Brushing Mindfully** - Brushing your teeth is the first activity you undertake each morning and the last thing you do at night. Make your first act of the day and your last act be one of mindfulness. Focus on the way your feet are standing on the floor, the way they are positioned, what you do with your free hand while the other brushes your teeth, and even focus on the brush strokes you take. What does the flavor of the toothpaste taste like? What about its texture? There are so many things aspects you can focus on with this mindful activity, and it's a great way to get your mindfulness practice in with an activity you already do anyway.

- **Mindfulness at Every Meal** - It's a blessing to have food on the table each night when so many people in the world go hungry. But how often do we stop to appreciate the meal we have instead of chewing down on auto-pilot as we aimlessly scroll through social media? Or even while we watch TV? Eat mindfully and with intention, savoring every bite, appreciating the way your meal tastes and smells. Eat slowly, listen to your body, and pay attention to when it tells you you're full. It will save you from future moments where you feel you're about to burst because you ate far too much.

- **Putting Your Phone Away** - When you commit to doing something, do it. Put your phone aside and leave the digital distraction behind. When was the last time you were completely focused on a conversation with someone without wondering what notification is beeped on your phone? We spend unhealthy amounts of time on our phone and its distracting us from being present in the moment. Learn to disconnect digitally and give your full attention to what you're supposed to be doing.

- **Showering Mindfully** - Yet another activity that is so routine we don't even think about what we do anymore happens in our daily shower sessions. Be mindful of the perfect water temperature and the way that it feels when that warm water hits your skin. Focus on the way your shampoo smells, how it feels as you lather it in your hair. Does your shower gel smell good? How does that scent make you feel? Listen to the sound of the water as it comes out of your shower head. There's so much to pay attention to once we start actively practicing mindfulness and we start to realize just how many things we previously did with little to no awareness at all. It's amazing how everything can be an activity in mindfulness.

- **One Mindful Minute** - No matter how busy you may be, you have at least one minute to spare. That's one way to think about it. Whenever you've got a moment to spare, set the timer on your phone for a minute, and spend that entire minute choosing something to be mindful about. This one-minute exercise is meant to strengthen your concentration over time, and everyone has a minute (or several minutes throughout the day) that they can spare.

• **Mindful Chores** - Running through your chores on auto-pilot most of the time? Every chore session can now be turned into a mindfulness training session. Instead of going through the motions hurriedly trying to get it over with, think about what you're doing every step of the way. Observe how many times your attention drifts and aim to do better next time.

• **No Multi-tasking** - A Jack of all trades is a master of none. Multi-tasking might give the illusion of being more efficient, but you won't be able to practice mindfulness when you're juggling several things at once. Your attention is split between the multiple tasks you're juggling at a time. If you want to start being more mindful, start by getting rid of your usual multi-tasking habit.

• **Mindfully Meditate Daily** - Now that you know just how beneficial meditation can be, the ideal scenario would be committing some time each day towards mindful meditation. It doesn't have to take up too much time, you can do it for as long as you can spare. Even 5-minutes a day of mindful meditation is better than nothing at all. 5-minutes can still be effective at initiating change. The biggest change of all sometimes starts with the smallest tweak in your habit. This could be that tweak.

• **Mindfulness Through Conversation** - The relationships we treasure the most are the ones we have managed to form a deep, meaningful connection with. These relationships can be enhanced even more when mindfulness is present in the mix. When you're mindful about the way you speak, the words you use, the way your body language reacts, and pay attention to the way the other person responds, your relationships improve because you're not just conversing for the sake of doing so. You're showing the other person that you care about the way they feel. That you empathize with them, relate to them, and you can see things from their point of view. This type of connection is so rare these days in a world where we seem to be distracted every minute. If it's not our phone's beeping and buzzing with the latest alert, it's some demanding task or other that requires attention. But when you put everything else aside and give your complete 100% attention to whomever you're speaking to, you instantly leave a positive impression just by showing them you cared enough to listen.

Some Final Pieces of Advice

Everyday mindfulness for stress management is a consistent practice. You now have just about everything you need to begin. You've seen that it is possible through the examples that have been discussed. All that's left is to get started, stay motivated, stay positive, and stick to it. Here's a quick recap of all the strategies you have covered in this book which will serve as useful reminders in your mindfulness practice for stress management:

• Start the morning being mindful as soon as you wake up. A good tip would be to start the day with a positive thought or affirmation as soon as the alarm rings and it's time to rise and shine.

• Practice exercising control over the kinds of thoughts you have. The more control you have over your thoughts, the less prone you will be to succumbing to stress.

• Stay alert and focus on the activities you undertake during the day. The more you concentrate on what you're doing, the less time you'll have to let your thoughts run wild.

• Avoid indulging in activities or situations that are only going to trigger your stress.

• Learn to adapt and be flexible to the situations and circumstances around you.

If things don't go as planned, tell yourself it's okay and adjust accordingly.

• When things start to feel too much, seek comfort in connecting with loved ones. Find someone you can trust and talk to them about how you feel. Sometimes it helps to just get it off your chest.

• Leave the past in the past where it belongs. You can't change what happened and dwelling on it is only going to rob you of your present joy. Use the past instead as a lesson for the future, learn from it.

• Find reasons to laugh and make yourself feel good.

• Learn to celebrate all the good things you have so you learn to worry less about the worst-case scenarios.

• Exercising regularly and keeping fit helps promote the release endorphins, which is the hormone you need to help you combat cortisol (stress hormone).

• Never be afraid to ask for help. Even the best people need help sometimes.

- Journaling is a good way to channel your emotions.

- Set intentions to give you a sense of purpose.

- Patience and acceptance are two very important qualities to need throughout this journey.

- Live in the moment. You know by now that obsessing and overanalyzing situations that haven't even happened will serve zero benefits.

- Learn to let things go in favor of being mindful of what you have instead. Complaining and worrying about the things you cannot change is not going to make a difference if you cannot change the situation anyway.

- Surround yourself with people who are positive, people who are motivated, people who are uplifting and people who can make you happy.

- Learn to say no and don't take on more than you can handle. It's not going to do your stress levels any favors by doing that.

Chapter 22: Emotional Meditation

As you probably have already noticed, there are several types of meditations. Included in these practices are often repeated exercises which include emotions, thoughts, and feelings. For instance, in the mindful eating meditation, you were instructed to pay attention to your thought and emotions as you ate. There are other meditations which also concentrate on the emotions, so perhaps it would be prudent to delve deeper into what is emotional intelligence.

Basically, at least according to the Oxford English Dictionary, emotional intelligence is defined as:

The capacity to be aware of, control and expresses one's emotions, and to handle interpersonal relationships judiciously and empathetically; emotional intelligence is the key to both personal and professional success.

Wow. It doesn't sound complicated, does it? Well, it is. There seems to be quiet a debate going on about whether emotional intelligence or IQ is the better indicator of life success. While the debate rages on, there are some truths that we can recognize.

There is little doubt that having the ability to understand and accept your emotions will help one gain success, in both their personal and professional life.

Managing emotions when under stress, top performers remain calm and in control of their emotions. In other words, they don't have a major meltdown.

Emotional meditation will improve emotional intelligence through the ability to remain in control.

IQ Verses EI

IQ is a score derived by taking a test of one's cognitive abilities that a person can manage in their job. It is proposed that you need a high IQ for top management, sciences, and professionals, while lower scorers work well in other areas.

IQ coupled with emotional intelligence (EI) sets good leaders apart and makes them better at their jobs. EI is NOT calmness, happiness, optimism, positivity, or any other personality trait. Instead, it's the individual's insight into understanding their emotions and how they can positively or negatively impact life and behavior skills. EI is really a process. It recognizes and assesses the situation and how to properly respond to it. EI is awareness.

When do we as humans acquire EI?

No, we are not born with it. It is a skill that starts when we are young, and children learn and ideally internalize these skills as they grow and develop. Children learn from those around them, so if they are in a dysfunctional family, for instance, it is highly likely their EI will be copied from their parents or other role models.

How do Mindfulness and Transcendental Meditation increase emotional intelligence?

On the Level of the Problem:

Mindfulness, the practice of training the mind to be 'in the present moment' and therefore becoming more aware of everything, including our emotions and habitual thought patterns, can begin the process of preventing further deterioration and the start of a recovery.

Addressing the Cause of the Problem:

Let's briefly talk about stress. Stress is not a thing. It is not something that happens to us. Instead, it is a deep psychosocial impression in the nervous system, usually caused by our reaction to past challenging events, which if not balanced, it puts us in a state of high emotional alert. Fight or flight sets in, and if prolonged, can cause extreme reactions to simple everyday things.

By simply becoming more aware of our emotions and therefore finding ways to balance them in a rational way, our reactions to events will be less severe, thereby decreasing the ingrained stress. We then can be calmer and less affected by external events. We remain calm and think clearly sour emotions do not control us. Rather, we control our emotions.

Being more aware of our emotions and thought patterns, we see situations more objectively and by choice, but gradually more spontaneously, react in a more intelligent and mature manner and no longer be controlled by dysfunctional patterns.

To put it even more simply: Good emotions makes us feel good. Negative emotions make us feel bad. One must also realize that emotions are transient. That is, they come and go. Yet they can have a powerful impact on our lives.

Knowing this is the first step in learning how to control the stress—and our reaction to it.

So, what is Emotional meditation? This meditation is as simple as the ones before it. You will be tasked to notice your emotions and acknowledge them without doing anything about them. You do this simply by sitting with your eyes closed and being aware of your emotions. Of observing then, the thoughts associated with them, and the feelings your body experiences with them.

All of these things are closely related. Different emotions are triggered by different things. You will come to know what those triggers are and by living alongside and not in them, you will change your perception of the situation and reaction to them

You will allow yourself to experience the emotions as they come, just being aware of whatever pops up. It may sound easy enough, but here is where problems can begin. Repressed emotions often come out in these sessions and make themselves known.

We are usually discouraged by society or family members from expressing these unpleasant emotions and there are even times when we aren't aware that they are there. Repressing or ignoring these unpleasant emotions really don't do anything with them. They don't leave. They just hang around and grow stronger and stagnant. They will then rear their ugly heads at the most inconvenient moment possible.

On the other hand, we often try to distract ourselves or numb our sensibilities from these often-painful emotions. We turn to things like eating, drinking, sex, shopping, social media and other potentially self-destructive behaviors as numbing agents which our psych then uses to protect us from harm. This really doesn't work, since all the emotions are just being pushed down and temporarily forgotten.

That is the dangerous part, well besides the determents to our health, but when we are caught up in any heightened emotion, even happy ones, the emotions all come banging on the door and we tend to make poor decisions which hopefully we'll live to regret later. We may say or do things that we don't mean.

This may be one of the best times to actually practice emotional meditation, for this makes us aware of the repressed emotions, the physical sensations that come with it, and the thoughts and self-talk we torment ourselves with.

When we do this, we can analyze the feelings, come to understand them, and ultimately soothe ourselves and go back to a fairly normal level of emotions.

There are times when we seem to get caught up in other's emotional turmoil, and mindful observation can help determine your feelings regarding the situation. This is important to people who are empaths, or those who are highly sensitive to the emotional states of others. It is imperative that these overly sensitive folks employ this technique to remain emotionally stable when dealing with others.

Eventually, as you progress, you will begin to notice the thoughts that are surrounding the emotions. The feelings, the sensations, and thoughts all come together, and you will gain new insight into your present emotional state, and it also gives you the power to control your responses.

Benefits of Emotional Meditation

The benefits of this practice are subtle but powerful. Following are a few examples:

Appreciation of good times. We've all heard how time flies, but challenging times seem to have the effect of slowing things down. Positive emotions allow you to savor the moment and appreciate all the positive things around you.

Managing Stress. It is very hard to be objective when you are emotionally charged. It is almost impossible to tell the difference in dynamics and actual occurrences. This is when most people blame others or play the same game. The more you practice this meditation the more you will be able to objectively view your emotions and separate them from the actual problem. If one is stressed, they are rarely calm or confident. That is the balanced state and stress is not part of it.

Accepting yourself and others: It is vital to accept yourself because your emotional health and habits are yours and yours alone. It is okay that you feel the way you do. Once you accept this for yourself, it is easier to accept it for other people too, and you will find that you have become more forgiving and open.

Ditching the mental baggage. We all have this trash. Grudges, anger, prejudice or dislike are just a few of the emotions we tend to hang onto. Bitterness and negativity pent up inside put a strain on emotional health. When we are able to let go of this rubbish, we don't have to carry it around with us anymore.

This does not mean accepting or applauding negative behaviors, but it does let go of the pain and negative emotions that go with it. It's like a ten-ton weight being lifted from our souls, and we are open to new experiences and opportunities.

Improved emotional self-regulation means we are able to express our feelings and emotions in a healthy and respectful way. While it is normal to have an occasional overreaction, you will be able to temporarily separate yourself from the emotion and see the big picture of the moment. Staying in the moment will decrease stress and increase emotional control.

Ability to identify your needs. Stress can do strange things. As adults, we sometimes feel things and don't understand what those emotional feelings are trying to tell us. With Emotional meditation, we analyze those feelings and are better able to understand what we need in order to meet those needs.

Equanimity and Emotional balance that comes from being able to see the bigger or whole picture. The more we are able to look outside and distance ourselves from the situation the more stable our emotions and thoughts will be. In turn, you will be able to make more rational and healthy choices and behaviors.

Equipment:

☐ Comfortable chair or cushion

☐ A quiet place where you won't be disturbed

☐ A timer. Again, if you use your phone be sure to set to vibrate and turn off notifications

☐ Meditation notebook, pen or pencil

How to start

We must remember that emotions and thoughts can change without warning and in the blink of an eye. Receiving bad news, watching the news, or any other catastrophic event can change a happy moment to one that sends us diving toward the bottom. The same can be sad for moments of sadness and grief, if a friend is seriously ill or passes away, or any other tragedy.

On the other hand, even these moments, you may find an opportunity to laugh or smile. There is nothing wrong with that. You should be kind to everyone, including yourself. That is what this meditation is about. The goal is not to dig up traumatic memories or seek out those dark things you have repressed. Here again, our goal is to be at the moment. In the here and now.

Take your emotions without judging them, analyzing them, or explaining them. They are what they are at this moment in time. This can be a challenge, to be sure. But, don't force it.

Our minds are really wonderous machines. As you acknowledge your emotions and thoughts, your mind will kick into autopilot and your subconscious will start immediately to work on a solution. You will find different thoughts coming, either about the solution or something else entirely. Trust your mind.

Conclusion

I am glad that you have taken this journey with me into Mindfulness Meditation. I have taken into account that you may never have experienced this before and have started you with the basics of relaxing and breathing as well as explaining the necessity for clearing the mind of thoughts that cause you anxiety, depression or even concern. The idea of Mindfulness is a very valid one, and it works. I know this from my experience and from my work with many people from all walks of life who have tried it and have indeed found that it was the answer to their problems.

When you first meditate, expect hesitation. Expect thoughts to be more important than letting go of them because it's something that you are not accustomed to. The best thing is that if you do it on a daily basis and it becomes a habit rather than taking a lot of effort, then you will learn from this that your body and mind have accepted this road in life and your subconscious mind has registered it as a habit that you don't need to plan all the time. You will really find it as natural as breathing and may even find yourself using mindfulness in all kinds of activities during the course of your life. It's okay to do that because all of the time that you are practicing mindfulness, you are telling those negative thoughts that you have no place for them in your life, and your mind switches over to seeing the cup half full instead of feeling that it is half empty.

I would ask readers to go back through the book and begin the exercises that I have suggested in the order that they were written. This is intentionally aimed at getting you ready for your mindfulness experience.

www.ingramcontent.com/pod-product-compliance
Lightning Source LLC
Chambersburg PA
CBHW072004070526
44583CB00015B/1321